CHARACTER QUEST

VOLUME TWO

STUDENT EDITION

Authors

SHARON R. BERRY, Ph.D., and OLLIE E. GIBBS, Ed.D.

LifeWay.

Published by
LifeWay Christian School Resources
127 Ninth Avenue North
Nashville, TN 37234-0182

Created and Developed by
Christian Academic Publications and Services, Inc.
Birmingham, Alabama

CharacterQuest, Volume 2
Table of Contents

INTRODUCTION

Who are you—way down deep inside where no one can see? What things are of greatest importance to you? To whom are you most committed? What is your nature and being? What are some things you would do, or not do, no matter the pressure given by others? What are you really like when no one is looking? All of these questions relate to the word "character."

The word "character" is defined as a distinguishing mark or distinctive quality. The sum of many of these unique traits defines the character of a person—who that person really is.

Name a person you know, perhaps a Steven or Jessica. You immediately think about that person's looks and personality. These are the features you can see in their appearance and behavior. However, if asked to describe someone's character, you would have to think deeper into what features are consistently shown in that person's life. Is Steven likely to cheat if given an opportunity, or can you really depend on him to be honest no matter what happens? Does Jessica's voice always sound a sour note, or is she basically cheerful and encouraging to others? The internal qualities that you observe daily in your friends make up their character. At the same time, the qualities they see in you every day define your character.

Who are you, really, way deep inside? Now is a good time to think about how others might describe you and how you might describe yourself. Look at the words in the following lists. Circle the top five positive traits you feel are generally true, or are likely to be said by others, about you.

kind	mature	hurtful to others
understanding	forgiving	impatient
truthful	cooperative	disorganized
sincere	self-disciplined	always late
courageous	persevering	undependable
loyal	prayerful	not a promise keeper
friendly	committed to Christ	not conscientious
respectful	shows initiative	unreliable
considerate	respectful	disobedient
joyful	orderly	always teasing
hard-working	careful	a show-off
conscientious	able to lead others	poor judgment
obedient	honest	immature
loving	prompt and on time	doesn't finish things
humble	selfish	prideful
tolerant	controlling	boastful
peaceable	unthankful	tattles
tender-hearted	hypocritical	gossips
determined	holds grudges	thinks sin is fun
wise	dishonest	wants to be first
generous	lazy	treats others unfairly
responsible	careless	selfish
merciful	untrustworthy	foolish
helpful	cheats	jealous
caring	cranky	insensitive
patient	never satisfied	stirs up trouble
faithful	complaining	gives up quickly
thankful	not a team player	argumentative
reverent	rude	encouraging

Obviously, these lists do not include everything, but they give you a good idea of the subject of this course: *Character Quest*. Your character is what you are when no one is looking. It is your inner heart from which all your personality and behaviors flow. Take a moment to read and write out the verse below.

Luke 6:45

_____

_____

_____

_____

_____

As a young teen, you are becoming more and more the person you want to be. Your parents' influence and control will lessen during these years as you decide what issues really matter to you. You are in the process of building the character which will in many ways determine the rest of your life.

Character really is important! It matters in the way you perceive yourself and the feelings you have about yourself. It is important with your parents, determining how much they can trust you and thus give you privileges to go and do things on your own. It counts with your teachers as they make assignments and give grades. And it matters with your friends! Are you loyal and caring? Can you be depended upon when trouble comes? Most importantly, character is significant with God! Are you becoming the person He wants you to be?

It is not unusual to pick up a newspaper and find stories on college students cheating, a local political leader caught in a lie, a congressman leading an impure life or even the head of a Christian organization stealing millions of dollars. Hot topics of conversation often focus on morality crises, ethical dilemmas and deteriorating societal values. Some people blame the government; others blame television. Teachers blame parents, and parents blame teachers. All agree that things must change dramatically with the next generation (that means you and your friends). All agree that development of godly character is critical in the world today.

For example, employers seeking workers to place in good jobs with high salaries made the following comments about young people and why they were not successful in business:

> *They are not dependable; they cannot take suggestions; they do not cooperate. If they finish one job, they expect someone to find them another instead of finding it for themselves. They are not punctual; they arrive late and begin to look at the clock before closing time. They are not loyal, criticizing and condemning unwisely and unjustly. They are untidy in their personal appearance.*

All of these reasons relate to the character of individuals—not how smart they are or how much they know. Thus good character is vital for your future.

The topics of ethics, morals, values and character are not new in education. Many notable people supported character eduction. Noah Webster, author of the first dictionary published in America, was a very committed Christian who greatly influenced our government. You can probably find a *Webster's Dictionary* in your classroom or library (greatly revised from the original one). It was Mr. Webster who said:

> *In my view, the Christian religion is the most important and one of the first things in which all children, under a free government, ought to be instructed. The moral principles and precepts contained in the Scriptures ought to form the basis of all our civil constitutions and laws. All miseries and evils which men suffer from (the vice, crime, ambition, injustice, oppression, slavery and war) proceed from their despising or neglecting the precepts contained in the Bible.*

Mr. Webster wrote a series of lessons entitled *Advice to the Young and Moral Catechism*. In them he spoke of obedience, love, curiosity of nature, faith, holiness, justice, service, humility, generosity, truth, gratitude, cheerfulness, industry and many other characteristics that were aimed at "learning those things which are to make you good citizens, useful members of society, and candidates for a happy state in another world (Heaven)."

Another name you will recognize is Benjamin Franklin. Remember that he discovered electricity by flying a kite in a storm. He was also a main figure in the first conventions in Philadelphia which framed the Constitution of the United States. When others could not agree and threatened to disband and go home to the colonies, Mr. Franklin proposed a day of prayer. God used him greatly to influence the foundations of government in the United States.

Benjamin Franklin is also well known for his efforts to establish a public school for common people who could not afford the elite private education of his day. The emphasis of this school was on the development of moral character. In fact, the teachers and principal met many months and concluded that, while subject matter was very important and desirable, character development was most needful. The virtues included were "unselfishness, self-control, honesty, economy, thrift, orderliness, the ability to reconcile differences, the ability to direct intelligently and cheerfully, an appreciation of art and beauty, and, most of all, a loving disposition, which is able to stand under many tests." Many schools based on the original model established by Benjamin Franklin are still in existence today.

A more current name you will recognize is Charles Lindbergh. He is famous for flying the first plane across the Atlantic Ocean. His comments demonstrate that he understood the importance of strong character.

I came to the conclusion that if I knew the difference between the right way to do a thing and the wrong way to do it, it was up to me to train myself to do the right thing at all times. So I drew up a list of character factors. At night I would read off my list of character factors, and those which I had fulfilled satisfactorily during the day I would mark

5

with a red cross. Those I had not been called upon to demonstrate that day would get no mark. But those character factors which I had actually violated each day, I would mark with a black cross. I began to check myself from day to day to compare my blacks and reds from month to month and year to year. I was glad to notice an improvement as I grew older.

Here are the "character factors" that Lindbergh recorded.

altruism	no sarcasm
ambition	no fault-finding
brevity in speech	no talking about others
concentration	no talking too much
calmness in temper	optimism
clean body	perseverance
clean speech	physical exercise
clean conduct	pleasant voice
cheerfulness	punctuality
courage	patience
courtesy	politeness
decisiveness	respect supervisors
determination	respect fellowman
economy	readiness to compromise
energy	recreation: manful not sinful
enthusiasm	self-esteem
firmness	self-control
faith	self-confidence
gracefulness	sense of humor
hopefulness	sleep and rest
industry	sympathy
justice	sincerity
moderateness	tact
modesty	thoroughness
neat appearance	unselfishness
no argument	

Character was important to many famous people as they achieved success in our world. Is character important to you?

Because moral values and character issues are of such concern in the world today, many businesses, colleges and schools have designed courses in which their employees or students study the development of these traits. Most of these courses have no Biblical basis for their subject matter. They simply say that fairness, truthfulness, concern for others, honesty, etc., are good for society. Therefore, people can learn the right thing and be motivated to do the right thing apart from any particular religion—especially one founded on the Bible. History has proven these thoughts wrong. Education can make a difference in the head of mankind but not in the heart of mankind.

A heart change is necessary if a person is to develop good character and live justly in the world. This is the meaning of 2 Corinthians 5:17: "Therefore, if anyone is in Christ, he is a new creation; old things have passed away; behold, all things have become new." From this change of heart and commitment to live in a new relationship with Jesus Christ, a person begins the process of Romans 12:2: "And do not be conformed to this world, but be transformed by the renewing of your mind, that you may prove what is that good and acceptable and perfect will of God."

Does this mean only Christians can develop good character? No, not at all. Some people using the name of Christ (Hitler, for one) have caused great harm in the world. On the other hand, many people live morally good lives in comparison to others (remember the rich young ruler). However, it is only the Christian who has a deep commitment to God, believes the Bible has given us everything needed for godliness and life, and has the Holy Spirit as a helper in conforming to the character of Jesus Christ.

All admirable character traits have their ultimate source and example in God, who is the Father of Light and Giver of every good and perfect gift. As we accept His Son Jesus and He begins to live His life in us, the character traits begin to naturally occur. They are not forced on us like an old coat that is too tight and heavy. Rather, they begin to grow within us as we daily commit ourselves to cooperate with the Holy Spirit. He teaches, leads, convicts and gives victory. This is a wonderful experience.

Character matters! This course has been designed to help you study this very important topic. It is one of two courses for your age group which focus on the development of admirable character. Each week you will consider a different character trait. You will study Biblical examples, definitions, and most important, you will learn how to include each character trait in your life. Hopefully, you will commit to learning as much as you can. But head knowledge is not the goal of your study. Your application of godly principles to everyday life is really the test of success. May God bless you as you follow the prescription of Peter.

> "Giving all diligence, add to your faith virtue, to virtue knowledge, to knowledge self-control, to self-control perseverance, to perseverance godliness, to godliness brotherly kindness, and to brotherly kindness love. For if these things are yours and abound, you will be neither barren nor unfruitful in the knowledge of our Lord Jesus Christ" (2 Peter 1:5–8).

INQUIRY-ACTION Intro.1

2 PETER 1:5–7

Start with _____

With _____ (or hard work)

add _____ .

Then add _____ ,

_____ ,

_____ ,

_____ ,

_____   _____ ,

and _____ .

INQUIRY-ACTION Intro.2

A LETTER TO ME

Date: _____

Dear _____,

After giving it some thought, the three character areas I would like to work on during this course are _____, _____, and _____.

I believe I can do this in the following ways:

_____

_____

_____

_____

_____

_____

_____

_____

With commitment to myself alone,

_____

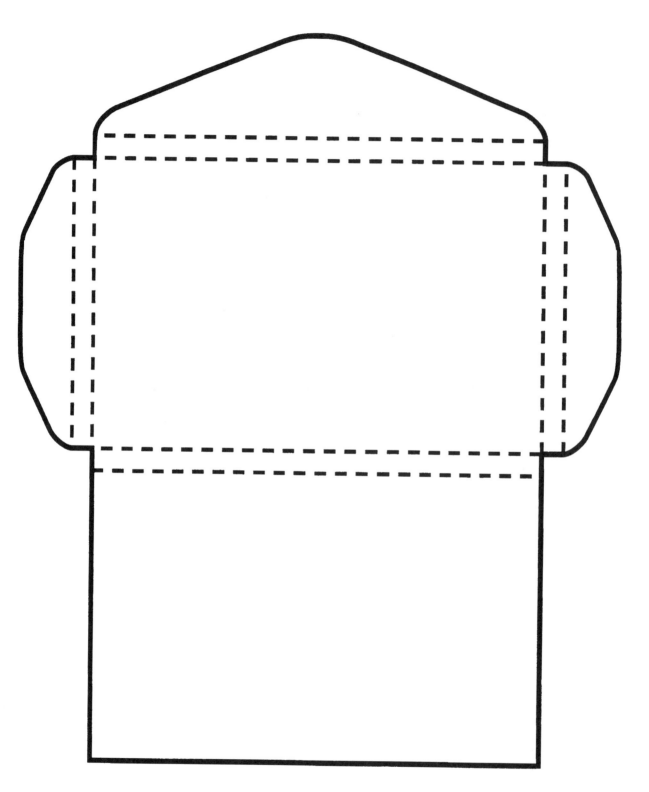

12

INQUIRY-ACTION Intro.3

CHARACTER SEARCH

```
Y T I L I M U H M R Y R X S S R E V E R E N C E M M G L A F
L N I N T E G R I T Y J K S E S W K B G C O M M I T M E N T
L O Q G V Q W X G O F W E E S R W I A P U R I T Y X V G T V
S E L F C O N T R O L N A E L N V R S L O V E A J J T N N C
J S F Y U V A E R T L L N F G B U I O D R K L S C H B Y E O
X Y S W C Y C G E U S E J F T O M E C E O E D J A E Z T M N
V L D V V N I N F H V S S K C K C N V E C M S N T T W I T T
V B Z D E V G Y N I R T E I I O D O U I K N K P K S V L N R
I V M I E L O H T O H V W N N O U I E B T F E L E B H I E O
N S T N N J M N S H F L D F I C F T Y T U A P I U C X B T L
V A E A Q E E V W M M N I Y C L E A V L M Y I B D B T I N L
P S I Q H T I A F U E D P W A D R R N Z L T H T T E I S O E
S H J V T F Y K K S E K N P V B H E I U O I S R I O B N C D
C H J A U C T A S N R E Y A R P S P D T S R R W A N Y O U S
K Z C J Z C L G C J X F O M G S U O J R Y U E I R M I P N P
J S F D O O A E D I L I G E N C E O F Y O T D G X E J S O E
M H K P R B Y M B Y T N E M N R E C S I D A A Y S V A E X E
G B O Y M Y O V M S Q H Z H O N E S T Y S M E R B A P R V C
P Y N F F Y L E N C O U R A G E M E N T J L L N N F G R T H
```

LOVE	LOYALTY	DISCERNMENT
WISDOM	HUMILITY	SINCERITY
OBEDIENCE	ORDERLINESS	PURITY
COURAGE	CONFIDENCE	MATURITY
ATTENTIVENESS	DILIGENCE	CONTROLLED SPEECH
FAITH	PRAYER	KINDNESS
RESPONSIBILITY	INTEGRITY	RESPECT
THANKFULNESS	PATIENCE	LEADERSHIP
HONESTY	FORGIVENESS	COMMITMENT
JOYFULNESS	INITIATIVE	SERVICE
SELF-CONTROL	CONTENTMENT	REVERENCE
	ENCOURAGEMENT	

INTEGRITY

Consistently Living According to the Truth

In March of 1942, the future of World War II did not look too promising for the American troops. This was especially true in the Pacific, where the Japanese seemed to be unstoppable. One island after another fell to the Imperial Forces of Japan. The enemy was now marching into the Philippines, confident that this multi-island empire would soon be under Japan's complete control.

Directing the Pacific battle strategy from his command post in the Philippines was the brilliant general, Douglas MacArthur. When it became obvious that the Japanese would soon overtake the islands, General MacArthur prepared to board a ship that would take him safely to Australia. As he stepped into the escape boat, he had only three parting words for the people of the Philippines:

I SHALL RETURN!

A little over 30 months later—October 20, 1944, to be exact—he stood once again on Philippine soil. In his first radio announcement, he declared, "This is the voice of freedom, General MacArthur speaking. People of the Philippines, I HAVE RETURNED!"

MacArthur kept his word. His word was as good as his bond. Regardless of the odds against him, including the pressures and power of enemy strategy, he was determined to make his promise good.

Today it is becoming increasingly difficult to find individuals who keep their word. As a result, the term "credibility gap" was coined. To say that something is "credible" is to say it is "capable of being believed." To refer to a "gap" suggests that there is an absence of trust, a "reason for doubt."

Jurors often have reason to doubt the testimony of a witness on the stand. Parents are finding it more and more difficult to believe their own children. Citizens frequently doubt the promises of politicians. Banks are finding it harder to believe that they will be paid back the money they have loaned. Unfortunately, the "credibility gap" is growing wider with each passing day. No longer do people do what they say they will do without a reminder, a warning or a threat.

Maintaining your integrity means that you must be faithful, uncompromising and pure. Listen to what the Scriptures say about the importance of your integrity:

> "When a man . . . takes an oath to obligate himself by a pledge, he must not break his word but must do everything he said" (Numbers 31:2 NIV).

> "It is better not to vow than to make a vow and not fulfill it"
> (Ecclesiastes 5:5 NIV).

> "O Lord, who may abide in Thy tent?
> Who may dwell on Thy holy hill?
> He who walks with integrity . . .
> And speaks truth in his heart" (Psalm 14:1–2 NAS).

How good are you at consistently living according to the truth? In other words, would those who know you best say that you have a "credibility gap"? Are you always faithful, uncompromising and pure in both your words and actions?

On a scale of 0 to 10 (0 = never and 10 = always), how would you rate yourself on the following questions?

1. When you say that you will meet someone at a certain place, at a certain time, do you?

2. When you say that you will pay someone back the money they loaned you by a certain time, do you?

3. When you tell someone they can depend on you to help them out, can they?

4. When you reply, "Yes, I'll pray for you," do you?

5. Certainly no one is perfect. But when you fail, do you admit it? Or, like many people, do you try to give excuses to cover your actions?

Beginning today, ask the Lord to help you consistently live according to the truth. Determine that you will be faithful, uncompromising and pure in both word and actions. When you fail, admit it and take responsibility for your behavior. This is the only pathway to integrity.

Remember, there is One Who has always lived a life of perfect integrity. He will always keep His Word. In fact, He's never broken one promise. There's no "credibility gap" with Him. Let Jesus be your partner in developing integrity.

INQUIRY-ACTION 19.1

INTEGRITY

Synonyms	Antonyms

INQUIRY-ACTION 19.2

I HATE HYPOCRISY

I think it's hypocritical when _____

_____

_____

_____

_____

_____

_____

The Biblical principle or passage that is related to this type of hypocrisy is:

_____

_____

_____

_____

_____

_____

_____

INQUIRY-ACTION 19.3

Action:	What does the world say?	What does the Word say?
gossip		
obeying parents		
telling dirty jokes		
Sports Illustrated swimsuit issue		
drugs, alcohol or tobacco		
greed		
attitude toward authority		
honesty		
lying		
discouragement / bitterness		

INQUIRY-ACTION 19.3 (CONTINUED)

laziness		
critical spirit		
anger		
worry		
conceit		

INQUIRY-ACTION 19.4

CHARACTERISTICS OF INTEGRITY FROM THE LIFE OF JOSEPH

In Genesis 39 we learn of Joseph's integrity as he faces the temptations of Potiphar's wife. As you study this passage, record examples of integrity under each of the following categories:

Faithfulness:

_____

_____

_____

_____

Uncompromising lifestyle:

_____

_____

_____

_____

Purity:

_____

_____

_____

_____

INQUIRY-ACTION 19.5

HOW DO I MEASURE UP?

As a class, identify a list of behaviors that are inconsistent with a Christian lifestyle and record them below. Then, at the space to the right, indicate whether or not each behavior is true in your life.

BEHAVIOR:	ALMOST ALWAYS	SOME- TIMES	ALMOST NEVER
1.			
2.			
3.			
4.			
5.			
6.			
7.			
8.			
9.			
10.			
11.			
12.			

INQUIRY-ACTION 19.5 (CONTINUED)

What should I do?

1. _____

_____

2. _____

_____

3. _____

_____

4. _____

_____

With God's help, I promise . . .

_____

_____

_____

_____   _____
Signature   Date

INQUIRY–ACTION 19.6   PSALM 25:4-5B, 21

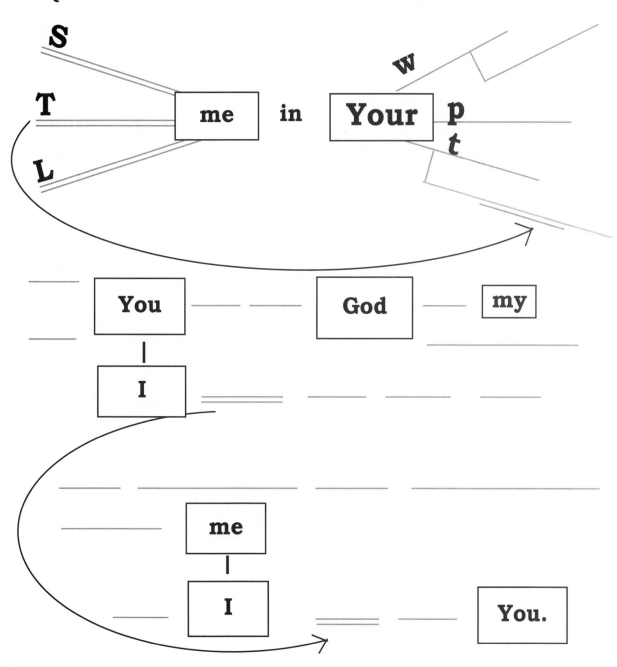

PATIENCE

Calmly Approaching Life's Challenges

What is the problem with the following statement? "Lord, give me patience . . . and I want it right now!"

If you said, "It doesn't happen that way," you're right. Getting patience is not like pulling up to your favorite fast-food restaurant and ordering a hamburger or picking up the telephone and ordering a pizza. Patience is not something that you can buy, get a degree in or inherit from someone else. Patience can only be developed as you calmly trust God to help you meet the experiences you face in life.

Think about those experiences you face on a regular basis—the ones that really irritate you. Get out your pencil and make a list of some of the things that "try" your patience. Here are a few suggestions to get you started.

cold food	long lines	crying babies	red lights
stuck zippers	doing dishes	talkative people	lack of skill
nosy siblings	homework	wrinkled clothes	waiting for your mom to drive the car

For most students, these items are a source of real irritation. You have probably already thought of a number of other things that you would like to add.

If it weren't for irritations we'd be very patient, wouldn't we? Unfortunately, we will never be completely free from irritations as long as we live on Earth. Never! It would be wise for each of us to accept this fact and look for a way to adjust to the irritations we face. With God's help, the irritations of life can become opportunities to develop patience.

God has given us a perfect illustration of how irritation and pain can make a difference in our lives. The example that God gives us is the oyster and its pearl.

Pearls are the product of pain. For some unknown reason, the shell of the oyster gets pierced, and a foreign substance—possibly a grain of sand—slips inside. Once that foreign irritant enters the oyster, all the resources within that tiny, sensitive oyster rush to the spot and begin to release healing fluids. Over a period of time, the wound is healed and the irritant is covered by a pearl.

A pearl is the result of the irritation. It is the result of a wound that has healed. Had there been no wounding or no irritation, there could have been no pearl. Of course, not all oysters are wounded. If you looked inside of them, you would find no pearl. These oysters are usable only as food.

Think about the list of irritations that you identified at the beginning of this lesson. Has it ever occurred to you that God uses these irritations to teach you patience and a more Christ-like character? Just as irritations form a pearl from a grain of sand, they form in us a godly patience that is evident to everyone.

The Bible teaches us that there are four types of "life situations" that God can use to develop patience in our lives. First, patience comes as a result of SUFFERING MISTREATMENT.

Have you ever been ridiculed because of your faith in Christ or your unwillingness to do something you know is wrong? The Bible is filled with examples of believers that suffered as a result of their faith. Peter reminds us to follow the example of the Lord Jesus Christ: "When they hurled their insults at him, he did not retaliate; when he suffered, he made no threats. Instead, he entrusted himself to him who judges justly" (1 Peter 2:23 NIV).

When we are suffering mistreatment as a result of our faith, the natural thing to do is to fight back. But notice what Peter says, " . . . He did not retaliate . . . He entrusted Himself to Him who judges justly." Patience comes as we endure the suffering and allow God to take care of the rest.

Patience can also come as a result of BEING PROVOKED. "Provoked" is not a word that we use every day. It means "to cause someone to become angry." If someone says something or does something that causes you to lose your temper, you have been provoked.

Do you remember the last time that someone made you very angry? Maybe someone broke a promise, repeated gossip about you or lied to you. What did you do, or what did you say? Those who have been provoked always look for ways to "get back at" the one who made them angry.

When someone has made you angry, the key to learning patience is to remember the words of James 1:19 (NIV), ". . . be slow to become angry." Rather than fighting back when someone angers you, ask God to help you control your actions and your words. Just as God was "slow to anger" when the Israelites sinned against Him, we must be "slow to anger" when others sin against us.

Are you sometimes irritated by the way others behave? Do you get upset by the way others dress or talk? If so, you need to learn patience as a result of TOLERATING SHORTCOMINGS.

If you haven't already noticed, everyone is different. Your classmates, sometimes even your closest friends, do not always agree with your opinions or share the same interests. Sometimes you might even wish that a certain student wasn't even in your school because that person doesn't "fit in" with everyone else.

When you criticize others for their shortcomings, you are showing an attitude of pride. You are saying to others, "I am better, smarter, more capable than this other person." Even if that is actually true, the Apostle Paul reminds us in 1 Corinthians 4:7 that the abilities we have are given to us by God. We have no reason to feel that we are any better than anyone else.

When the shortcomings of others begin to irritate us, the Bible teaches us to "bear with one another in love" (Ephesians 4:2–3). In other words, we are going "to put up with" the faults of others in order to maintain unity among believers.

Remember, as Christians we are commanded to love one another. If that is true in your life, you will overlook the shortcomings of those around you.

Patience can be learned as a result of WAITING ON GOD. Do you remember the quote at the beginning of this lesson? "Lord give me patience . . . and I want it right now!" That's the way many of us approach God's timetable for our lives.

Abraham's long wait for the birth of his son, Isaac, is the perfect Biblical illustration of the need for patience when we wait for God's timing. Abraham tried everything he could think of to speed up the timetable. But all of his efforts failed. The birth of Isaac would happen according to God's timetable.

God's method of teaching us patience is through adjustment to irritation. Which of these four experiences is God using to teach you patience? Are your classmates mistreating and making fun of you because of your Christian testimony? Have you been provoked to anger because of lies and gossip? Do the habits and shortcomings of others bother you? Is God taking too long to answer your prayers?

Remember, without the irritation of the sand inside the oyster, the pearl would never have appeared. In the same way, God can never teach us patience unless we experience the irritations of life. The next time something irritates you, remember the oyster and the pearl. Wait patiently on the Lord. He will use that irritation to strengthen your character and draw you closer to Him.

INQUIRY-ACTION 20.1

"PATIENCE" QUESTIONNAIRE

In preparation for tomorrow's class, ask the following questions to an adult.

1. What makes you the most impatient?

2. When you are impatient in this area, what kind of problems does it cause for you?

INQUIRY-ACTION 20.2

RESEARCH AND REPORT

Assignment: _____

What is the background of this story?

How was patience shown by the main character in this story?

What is the most important lesson about patience that we should learn from this story?

How will we present this information in the class?

INQUIRY-ACTION 20.3

OUR GOD IS A PATIENT GOD

Using both sides of this sheet, write a letter to your teacher in order to convince him or her that "Our God Is a Patient God." You must use Biblical passages and events as the basis for your argument. Be sure to make an application to daily life.

Dear _____,

_____

_____

_____

_____

_____

_____

_____

_____

INQUIRY-ACTION 20.3 (CONTINUED)

_____

_____

_____

_____

_____

_____

_____

_____

_____

_____

_____

_____

Signature

INQUIRY-ACTION 20.4

IDENTIFYING INCONSISTENCIES

During the past week, how well have you maintained integrity in your life? How well have you shown patience? In other words, what areas of inconsistency have you identified in your own life during the past week?

In the space provided below, explain areas of personal inconsistency that you have observed in the past week. Then describe what you are going to do to make sure that you are consistent in that area in the future.

Inconsistent Behavior: _____

_____

My Plan for the Future:_____

_____

_____

Inconsistent Behavior: _____

_____

My Plan for the Future:_____

_____

_____

Inconsistent Behavior: _____

_____

My Plan for the Future:_____

_____

INQUIRY-ACTION 20.5

COLOSSIANS 1:10–11 (NKJ)

Work from the end to the beginning. Restore all the vowels and write the verses.

yjhtwgnrffsgnldncntpllrf
rwpsrlgsHtgndrccthgmllhtw
dnhtgnrtsdGfgdlwnkhtngnsrcndn
krwdgyrvnlftrfgnbmHgnslpyllf
drLhtfyhtrwklwymythT

FORGIVENESS

A Free Gift That You Can Give

Little Tommy was very upset with his brother. Before he said his prayers, Tommy's mother said to him, "Before you go to sleep, I want you to forgive your brother." But Tommy had no desire to forgive his brother. "No, I won't forgive him," he told his mother.

Tommy's mother continued to talk to him about forgiveness. But Tommy was determined not to forgive his brother. Finally, his mother said, "What if your brother were to die tonight? How would you feel if you knew you had not forgiven him?"

"All right, I'll forgive him; but if he's still alive in the morning, I'm going to get him for what he did to me!"

It is pretty clear that little Tommy does not understand the true meaning of forgiveness. Yet his response may not be too different from the one you or your friends might make.

The word "forgive" means to "give away." Suppose you lend your best friend some money. A couple of weeks later you decide that your friend doesn't need to pay you back. You inform your friend that you are going to "forgive the debt." What you have done is "give away" your right to ever ask for that money again. Once the act of forgiveness has taken place, the debt is forgotten forever!

At some time in everyone's life, the need to forgive or be forgiven becomes necessary. This was certainly true in the life of Andrew Jackson, the seventh President of the United States. President Jackson was one of the most unusual—and most popular—leaders our country has ever had.

President Jackson grew up fighting—and hating! At the top of his "hate list" were the British and the Indians. During the American Revolution, the British soldiers killed his two brothers and his mother. He was made a prisoner of war at the age of 14.

At the end of the Revolution, Jackson was released from prison camp. He turned his attention to the settling of the West, which at that time extended only as far as the state of Tennessee. It was during these years that he saw firsthand how his countrymen were being slaughtered by the Indians. He felt nothing but hatred for the British and the Indians for what they had done to his family and his friends.

It was during the War of 1812 that Jackson became a national hero. Stories about his bold attacks on the Indians and British troops were repeated in every small town and village in this young nation. Jackson added to his fame by putting down a Seminole Indian uprising in Florida in 1818, followed by his appointment as Military Governor of this newly acquired territory.

Because of his growing popularity, he decided to run for the Presidency in 1824. Although it was a close race, he was defeated by John Quincy Adams. However, four years later he ran again and won by a large majority.

There were many leaders in government who questioned Jackson's ability to be President. Unlike the Presidents who had preceded him, he did not come from a wealthy family or a famous college. He was a frontiersman. He had grown up on the battlefield.

Jackson proved the doubters to be wrong. He was a strong leader who remained popular with the people throughout his two terms in office. Yet it is what happened in the closing years of his life that is most remarkable.

He realized that he was a sinner who needed forgiveness and accepted Jesus Christ as his personal Savior. As a result of this decision, he had to make what he considered the most difficult decision of his life. He had to forgive his enemies.

It was one thing to forgive his political enemies, but to forgive those who had killed his family and friends was a different matter. In the end, Andrew Jackson put aside his hatred and stood before his pastor and congregation and confessed his faith in Christ. As one historian said, Andrew Jackson was one who "dared to do anything that was right to do."

Forgiveness is the right thing to do. Have you ever stopped to think about the price that you pay when you are unwilling to forgive someone? Whenever you hold on to anger because of what someone else has done to you, you are actually punishing yourself. The grudge that you hold against that other person affects your emotions and your happiness.

First of all, remember that God has forgiven you. Suppose you break the law and you are caught. Because of your crime, the judge fines you $1,000. What are you going to do? You know you have committed the crime, but you don't have the money to pay the fine. All of a sudden, the judge pulls out his checkbook and pays the fine that you owe. Your debt has been paid. You have been completely forgiven!

God has done this for us, only in a much greater way. The payment that He demanded for our sin was death. But God provided a way of forgiveness for us. "Therefore let it be known to you, brethren, that through this Man is preached to you the forgiveness of sins" (Acts 13:38).

The most important forgiveness in this world is the forgiveness that God has provided for us through His Son, Jesus Christ. If you do not know the Lord as your Savior, you will never understand the full meaning of forgiveness.

Because God has forgiven us, the next step we must take is to forgive others. Our fellowship with God is affected when we refuse to forgive others. "For if you forgive men their trespasses, your heavenly Father will also forgive you. But if you do not forgive men their trespasses, neither will your Father forgive your trespasses" (Matthew 6:14–15).

Do you have difficulty forgiving others? If so, you might not really understand what it means to forgive.

- Forgiveness is denying that you've been hurt. NOT!
- Forgiveness is accepting and condoning the wrong others have done. NOT!
- Forgiveness is a response when others say they are sorry and try to make things right. NOT!
- Forgiveness happens only the first couple of times someone does wrong. NOT!
- Forgiveness is explaining away the wrong behavior of someone toward you. NOT!
- Forgiveness is understanding why a person has acted in a certain way toward you. NOT!

Forgiveness is choosing to release others from debts we feel they owe us because of the hurt they have caused in our lives. Forgiveness is a "free gift that we can give." We are obligated to give it only because God forgave us.

Who in your life do you need to forgive? Don't allow bitterness to control your life as a result of your unwillingness to forgive someone else. Forgiveness is the right thing to do! Forgiveness is necessary for your personal happiness as well as for your relationship with your Heavenly Father to be blessed.

INQUIRY-ACTION 21.1

NEWS SEGMENT FORMAT

ANNOUNCER: (Introduces the segment and segues to reporter.)

_____

_____

_____

_____

_____

REPORTER: (Briefly tells what has happened; can segue to an interviewer
               or bring eyewitnesses in to give reports.)

_____

_____

_____

_____

_____

INQUIRY-ACTION 21.1 (CONTINUED)

EYEWITNESSES: (Two or three can give their perspective and answer questions
                    from interviewer or reporter.)

_____

_____

_____

_____

_____

REPORTER: (Summarizes what has happened and why it's so amazing.)

_____

_____

_____

_____

_____

ANNOUNCER: (Thanks the reporter and challenges the audience to consider
                the place of forgiveness in everyday life.)

_____

_____

_____

_____

_____

INQUIRY-ACTION 21.2

PRINCIPLES OF FORGIVENESS

Hebrews 12:14–15

• God is the Author of forgiveness.

Psalm 103:2–3, 8–12

• Christ's death brought God's forgiveness to us.

Romans 4:25; 5:8; 6:23; 8:1–2

• On the basis of God's forgiveness, we are commanded to forgive others.

Matthew 5:22; 1 John 3:15

• The requirement to forgive is unlimited.

Ephesians 4:32

• Forgiveness brings joy and gratitude.

Romans 12:17–21; 1 Timothy 5:24

• Lack of forgiveness demonstrates hatred.

Luke 17:3–4

• Lack of forgiveness can hinder God's forgiveness.

Luke 7:47

• Unforgiveness can produce bitterness which can destroy a person from within.

Mark 11:25–26

• Judgment for wrong action belongs to the Lord. He will settle the debt.

INQUIRY-ACTION 21.3

A PROPER RESPONSE

Offense	Inappropriate Response:	Appropriate Response:	Difference Between the Two:
Talked back to parent	"I'm sorry you feel I sassed you."	"I am sorry I didn't respect you as my God-given authority. Will you forgive me?	The correct confession deals with the basic sin and asks that the person be forgiven, not the offense.
Cheated on a test in school	"I'm sorry that I was caught copying Jim's test."	_____ _____ _____ _____ _____ _____ _____	The inappropriate response reveals no regret over cheating.
Went to a late afternoon event without permission	"I'm sorry I didn't tell you I was going out."	"I'm sorry I selfishly considered only what I wanted at the moment. You're in charge, not me. Will you forgive me?"	_____ _____ _____ _____ _____ _____ _____ _____

INQUIRY-ACTION 21.3 (CONTINUED)

Complained about going on vacation	"I'm sorry you're getting angry."		The inappropriate response makes the person offended seem wrong for being angry.
Told "dirty jokes"	"If I offended you, I'm sorry."		
Told a secret	"I'm sorry I couldn't keep your secret."	"I have broken my promise to you and I'm sorry for my lack of self-control and dishonesty. Will you forgive me?"	
Made fun of a fellow student	"I'm really sorry that we made fun of you."		

INQUIRY-ACTION 21.4

ASKING FORGIVENESS

We must be willing to forgive others, even when they have offended us. In the space provided below, make a list of those areas in which you should forgive someone else. Once you have done that, go back to your list and star the three most difficult areas for you to forgive.

1. _____

2. _____

3. _____

4. _____

5. _____

6. _____

7. _____

8. _____

9. _____

10. _____

INQUIRY–ACTION 21.4 (CONTINUED)

FORGIVENESS ACTION PLAN

As you prepare your personal "Forgiveness Action Plan," write the following information.

Individuals I Have Offended:	Individuals Who Have Offended Me:
Individual: I should . . .	Individual: This individual should . . .
Individual: I should . . .	Individual: This individual should . . .
Individual: I should . . .	Individual: This individual should . . .
Individual: I should . . .	Individual: This individual should . . .

INQUIRY-ACTION 21.5

COLOSSIANS 3:13–15

INQUIRY-ACTION 21.6

BOTTOM-LINE QUESTIONS

1. Why is forgiveness a fundamental principle of Christianity?

_____

_____

_____

_____

2. Why is forgiveness not simply saying "I'm sorry"?

_____

_____

_____

_____

3. How will your life be affected if you are not willing to forgive someone for an offense committed against you?

_____

_____

_____

_____

INQUIRY–ACTION 21.6 (CONTINUED)

4. Without writing out the person's name, whom do you need to forgive?
In the space provided, write out . . .

   a) how that person has offended you.

   _____

   _____

   _____

   b) why it will be hard to forgive that person.

   _____

   _____

   _____

   c) why it is important for you to forgive that person today.

   _____

   _____

   _____

   d) the steps you will take to show forgiveness of that person.

   _____

   _____

   _____

INITIATIVE

Not Waiting to Be Told What to Do

When disaster strikes anywhere in the world, often the first group to respond with food and supplies is the Red Cross. The Red Cross, founded in 1863, was an attempt to provide care for those wounded in the many ongoing battles throughout Europe.

The United States was not one of the fourteen countries involved in the founding of the International Red Cross. However, that would soon change because of the efforts of Clara Barton and her commitment to Christ.

Miss Barton, a native of Massachusetts and a schoolteacher for 17 years, always had a desire to help others. Whether it was the students in her classroom or the neighbors down the street, Clara Barton cared about those in need.

It was the outbreak of the Civil War in 1861 that changed the life of Clara Barton—and the direction of the Red Cross—forever! In April of 1861 Miss Barton was at the train station in Washington, D.C., when many wounded men from the Sixth Massachusetts Militia arrived. She immediately went to the hospital to nurse the wounded.

Much to her surprise, no one was prepared to care for so large a number. It was at this point that Clara Barton took charge of the situation. She contacted relatives and friends, asking for donations of food and bandages. Soon she had to rent a warehouse to store all of the supplies that had been given.

As the war spread, Miss Barton left the safety of the hospital to go to the troops on the battlefield. Often, she would care for the wounded right behind the battle lines. It was not long before the soldiers had given her the name, "Angel of the Battlefield."

At the end of the four-year war, Clara Barton went to Europe for a well-earned rest. It was at this time she met representatives of the International Red Cross. As they shared their experiences, she was asked why the United States did not work with the organization. Her only reply was that the Red Cross was not known in America—a fact that was soon to change!

It took Clara Barton five years to convince Congress to establish a branch of the International Red Cross in the United States. She found herself the head of a group that had no income, no employees and no office. And, since America had no wars, the group actually had nothing to do. It was then that she realized that the Red Cross should be involved in disasters other than war: floods, hurricanes, earthquakes, fires and any hardship that caused suffering. It was not long before the Red Cross was known as the nation's volunteer relief organization.

At her retirement in 1904, Clara Barton was honored with the title, "America's Greatest Heroine." But in her closing remarks, she gave God the glory for her accomplishments when she said, "One must never think of anything except the need and how to meet it. Then God gives the strength, and the thing that seemed impossible is done."

Initiative—not waiting to be told what to do—was demonstrated throughout Clara Barton's career. When she saw a need in her classroom or her neighborhood, she did whatever she had to do to meet that need. When she learned that the troops did not have the proper medical supplies or personal care, she took the initiative to get what they needed. She even went to the battlefield herself to care for the wounded. When she realized that the Red Cross was unknown in America, she went on a campaign to inform the nation. Miss Barton knew that God would give her the strength to accomplish His will.

The Bible records the stories of many individuals who took the initiative under very difficult circumstances. We will look at three of them. The first was the prophet Samuel. Until the time of Samuel, the nation of Israel had been ruled by judges for over 400 years. As a result, the work of the priests and the teaching of God's Word had been neglected.

Samuel took the initiative to organize the "school of the prophets." He trained a group of dedicated men to go throughout the country to re-establish the sacrifices, worship services and the teaching of God's Word. As a result of Samuel's initiative, the nation of Israel turned from their worship of idols and returned to their worship of God.

Our second example of initiative is Josiah, who became king when he was only eight years old. Because of the wickedness of the kings that had ruled before him, Israel was involved in all types of pagan worship. God and His Word had been neglected. Josiah removed the false priests who were in the Temple and destroyed the idols. He appointed religious leaders who were faithful to God and once again required the reading of God's Word. His reform began in Judah but soon spread throughout Israel. His leadership was so great that even the surrounding nations were influenced by his reforms.

Nehemiah's life provides a third excellent illustration of initiative. As a result of Israel's sin, the nation had been taken captive by Babylon. For many years the nation was in exile. Finally, under the leadership of Ezra, the Israelites were allowed to return home. A number of years later Nehemiah, who held a high position of leadership in the Persian court as cupbearer to King Artaxerxes, asked if he could visit Jerusalem. He was granted permission to return.

Upon arriving in Jerusalem, Nehemiah was shocked by what he saw. Even though the Israelites had lived in the city for many years, Jerusalem had not been rebuilt. The walls had not been repaired, God's Law was being ignored, worship had not been restored and the Sabbath was not being observed.

Nehemiah took the initiative to begin rebuilding the walls. Although he faced many obstacles throughout this rebuilding process, God honored his leadership. After many years of hard work, the walls were rebuilt, God's Law was once again obeyed by the people, worship was restored and the Sabbath was observed.

When there is a job to be done, how do you respond? Is your first thought, "That's not my job; someone else is going to have to do it!"? Or do you think, "I like to be asked before I tackle a job"? Neither response characterizes a person with initiative. Nor do these responses bring glory to God. James 4:17 reminds us that to know to do good but fail to do it is sin. Believers are to act on their faith.

Are there students in your school who have no friends? Is there a task at home that no one seems to want to do? Have you ever invited someone to attend your Sunday School class? These are just a few examples of areas where you can take the initiative.

Clara Barton said it best: "One must never think of anything except the need and how to meet it. Then God gives the strength. . . ." God wants us to respond when we know a job needs to be done. He will give the strength—and the blessing—if we will only take the initiative and do what we know is right.

INQUIRY-ACTION 22.1

In personal commitment to the Lord and corporate commitment to fellow believers, I plan to focus on the following three areas.

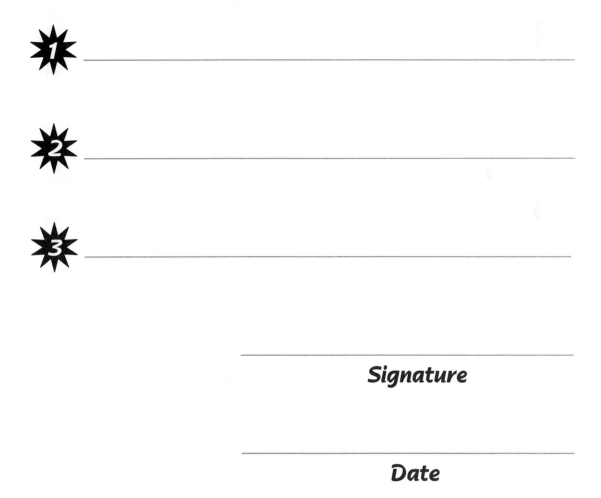

1 _____

2 _____

3 _____

_____

Signature

_____

Date

INQUIRY-ACTION 22.2

Issue: _____

_____

_____

How should I become involved? _____

_____

_____

What would probably prevent me from becoming involved? _____

_____

_____

Who is responsible to take the first step? _____

_____

_____

Inquiry-Action 22.3

Some things I see around school that need to be done.

1. _____

_____

_____

2. _____

_____

_____

3. _____

_____

_____

INQUIRY–ACTION 22.4

Check out some admonitions for initiative and warnings against inactivity, being a sluggard or being idle and lazy. Work with a partner or small group to summarize these verses.

James 4:17 _____

1 Timothy 5:13 _____

Proverbs 10:5 _____

Ecclesiastes 9:10 _____

Matthew 25:14–29 _____

Proverbs 20:4 _____

James 2:15–17 _____

Proverbs 3:27–28 _____

Hebrews 6:11–12 _____

Proverbs 6:6–11 _____

Inquiry-Action 22.5

Draw a line from footprint to footprint to show the progression of words.

Brethren

do

myself

to

I

not

count

have

thing

one

but

apprehended

I

forward

to

those

reaching

do

things

which

forgetting

and

behind

ahead

things

which

are

those

are

Philippians
3:13

CONTENTMENT

Finding Complete Happiness in What God Provides

Are you getting the message? The advertisers who bought commercial TV time for the 1998 Super Bowl in San Diego sure hope so. They paid $50,000.00 a second to have the opportunity to convince you that their product was the best.

Manufacturers and merchants spend billions of dollars each year to get us to buy their products. When you want something cold to drink, they want you to think of their product. If you have a craving for something chocolate, it is their particular brand that they want you to buy.

Take a moment and think about some of the advertisements you've seen today. You don't have to go far for examples. There are commercials on the radio and television, sales ads in the newspapers and magazines, and billboards along the highway. Although these advertisers are selling many different things, they have the same message. They are trying to convince you that you need their product!

But advertising is more than selling you a certain product. It also wants to convince you that the product you are now using is inferior. A successful advertiser will first make you dissatisfied with what you are now using. Once the "seed of dissatisfaction" has been planted, the advertiser will sing the praises of its product.

Advertisers clearly understand two important principles of human nature: People want to be happy, and people are always dissatisfied about something in their lives. Advertisers are quick to point out that if you own a "certain" sports car, go to a "certain" theme park on vacation or own a "certain" pair of jeans, you will be happy.

It is this "disease of dissatisfaction" that is the focus of this week's lesson. What do you want, right now, that you don't have? Is there a certain item of clothing that you really want but cannot afford? Are you dissatisfied with the color of your hair? Do you wish you were taller, stronger, faster? If you cannot find complete happiness in what God has provided, you will not be able to experience the joy of contentment.

The story of Israel's bondage in Egypt is familiar to almost everyone. What do you think it would have been like to live in bondage to the Egyptians for 400 years? The Israelites had no place to call their own. As slaves, they were forced to do whatever the Egyptians demanded. They weren't even allowed to worship their own God.

Finally God sent Moses to deliver the people from the hands of the Egyptians. At first the Pharaoh would not let them leave. But God showed His power when He punished the Egyptians with the Ten Plagues. Pharaoh finally admitted defeat and let the Israelites go. What a day that must have been as the nation of Israel left the city of Pharaoh.

God was with His people. A pillar of cloud led them by day, and a pillar of fire led them at night. The people of Israel saw God's power at work. Certainly they would never doubt Him again.

However, in spite of all that God had done, the people soon became dissatisfied with His provision for them. The journey through the Wilderness had become long and hard. They were dissatisfied with the route God had directed them to take, and they were dissatisfied with the food that God had provided. According to Numbers 14:2, the people were so unhappy they wished that they had been left in Egypt to die. They had already forgotten the wondrous miracles that God had performed. The "disease of dissatisfaction" had set in.

As long as the nation of Israel was unable to find complete happiness in what God had provided, the people would never experience contentment. Their lack of contentment soon caused them to sin against God.

Being content is just as important for us today. The Apostle Paul understood this important principle when he said, "Not that I speak in regard to need, for I have learned in whatever state I am, to be content: I know how to be abased, and I know how to abound. Everywhere and in all things I have learned both to be full and to be hungry, both to abound and to suffer need" (Philippians 4:11–12).

In this verse Paul reminds us that we must learn contentment in two areas: our possessions and our position. In one of the strongest statements in the New Testament, Jesus warns us about being content with our possessions. He says in Luke 12:15, "Take heed and beware of covetousness, for one's life does not consist in the abundance of the things he possesses."

God knows that there are many "things" in this world that will tempt us. As a result, we often spend our time trying to obtain these "things" rather than serving Him. As Jesus said in the Sermon on the Mount, "you cannot serve God and money."

Are you content with what God has provided for you and your family? Are you dissatisfied because your friends have material "things" that you don't have? Why not make a list of all of the "things" that you wish you had. Then ask the Lord to help you become less attracted to the "things" on your list and more devoted to Him. For the next month keep the list with you as a reminder of the "things" that are keeping you from complete contentment.

Do either of the following statements describe your life? "I always want to be the leader" or "I'm just a nobody; God can't use me." If either of these attitudes are true in your life, you have not learned how to be content with your position.

In Romans 12:6, Paul reminds us that God has given gifts to every believer: ". . . we have gifts differing, according to the grace that is given to us." Our duty is not to decide what we want to be or to do, but to obediently follow the Lord wherever He leads us.

Contentment with position will only come when we are where God wants us to be. Whether you are the captain of the team or the president of your class, if you are not in that position because God wants you there, you will not experience contentment!

Contentment is not something you learn overnight. It takes time. The pathway to contentment begins when you realize that the possessions and positions of this world will not satisfy you. By focusing on God's goodness to you and the blessings He has provided, you find contentment that only He can give.

Isn't it time to start down the pathway to contentment? Ask God to forgive you for the "seeds of dissatisfaction" that are present in your life today. This is the first step to contentment. Remember, ". . . godliness with contentment is great gain" (1 Timothy 6:6).

Inquiry-Action 23.1

1 Timothy 6:6–11

Now godliness with contentment is great gain.

For we brought nothing into this world,

and it is certain we can carry nothing out.

And having food and clothing, with these we shall be content.

But those who desire to be rich fall into temptation and a snare,

and into many foolish and harmful lusts

which drown men in destruction and perdition.

For the love of money is a root of all kinds of evil,

for which some have strayed from the faith in their greediness,

and pierced themselves through with many sorrows.

But you, O man of God, flee these things

and pursue righteousness, godliness, faith, love, patience, gentleness.

INQUIRY-ACTION 23.1 (CONTINUED)

QUESTIONS

1. _____

_____

_____

_____

2. _____

_____

_____

_____

3. _____

_____

_____

_____

4. _____

_____

_____

_____

INQUIRY-ACTION 23.2

CONTENTMENT RATING SCALE

List below those areas in which you may find it difficult to be content. For each item, rate yourself from 1 (completely unhappy) to 5 (totally content).

Area to be rated	Completely unhappy				Totally content
1. Having enough money to spend	1	2	3	4	5
2. My personal looks	1	2	3	4	5
3. My ability to earn grades in school	1	2	3	4	5
4. My popularity	1	2	3	4	5
5. My skills in sports	1	2	3	4	5
6. My family situation	1	2	3	4	5
7. Having my own room	1	2	3	4	5
8. Having a family car	1	2	3	4	5
9. _____	1	2	3	4	5
10. _____	1	2	3	4	5

Based on the items listed above, select one of your weakest areas to work on in the coming week: _____

INQUIRY-ACTION 23.3

God wants me to be content because _____

_____

_____

_____

_____

To increase this characteristic in my life, I need to _____

_____

_____

_____

_____

My prayer and commitment are _____

_____

_____

_____

_____

_____
Signature

_____
Date

INQUIRY-ACTION 23.4

PERSONAL DISAPPOINTMENT

There are times when all of us are deeply disappointed or unhappy. In spite of our sorrow, God uses these times to teach us many valuable lessons.

Identify a time in your life when you experienced great disappointment or unhappiness.

_____

_____

_____

Explain why you were disappointed and how it affected you.

_____

_____

_____

Based on what you have learned so far this week, how will you respond to times of disappointment and discontentment in the future?

_____

_____

_____

INQUIRY-ACTION 23.5

1 TIMOTHY 6:6–8

3 A	2 B	6 C	2 F	3 G	1 H

Inquiry-Action 23.5 (CONTINUED)
1 Timothy 6:6–8

4 I	3 N	1 O	1 S	2 T	6 W

ENCOURAGEMENT

Compassion Put into Action

Millions of Jews died in the German concentration camps during World War II. All of these captives were forced to bear the hardships of the camps, but not all were forced to die in the horrific gas chambers or at the hands of the Nazis. Unlike the millions of Jews, Elizabeth Pilenko went to her death by choice.

Her story is one of caring, encouragement and love for others. Although reared in a wealthy family in Russia, she had compassion on the poor she saw all around her. Throughout her early years she smuggled food, clothes and toys to children who had none and spent her time teaching the poor to read and write.

Not wanting to participate in the Revolution, in 1923 she left Russia to live in Paris. She was eventually able to save enough money to open a small hospital to care for the sick and for orphans. She often said that her greatest joy was to be an encouragement to others.

But her life changed dramatically after the start of World War II. The German Army over-ran most of Europe. France was placed under German military rule. It was then that Elizabeth Pilenko made a decision that would threaten her life. She began hiding Jews in her hospital, keeping them from Nazi soldiers and certain death.

It was not long before she was discovered. Along with the Jews she was hiding, she was sent to one of the dreaded German concentration camps. In addition to their hard work, prisoners were starved, tortured and shot. Some prisoners were sent to the "bath houses," a fancy name for the gas chambers. Although not a Jew, Elizabeth Pilenko experienced the same hardships as her fellow prisoners.

Because she had hidden Jews in her hospital, she had been sentenced to the camp. But because she was not a Jew, she was not sentenced to the gas chamber. As the years passed, she continued to bring whatever care and encouragement she could to those around her. Even the guards had respect for her testimony among the prisoners.

It was a cold winter morning in 1945 when women prisoners were once again being lined up outside the gas chamber. In a few moments they would be ushered inside, with no hope of ever coming out alive. All of a sudden a young girl began scream-ing with fear. Elizabeth ran and put her arms around the crying child. "Don't be afraid. I will come with you." As she entered the death chamber with the young girl, Elizabeth Pilenko continued to do what she had done all of her life: she brought comfort and encouragement to others.

Elizabeth Pilenko understood the importance of Proverbs 16:24: "Pleasant words are like a honeycomb, sweetness to the soul and health to the bones." God used her to provide words of encouragement to those who were disappointed, discour-aged or scared.

Have any of your friends ever told you that they were discouraged or unhappy with their lives? Discouraged people need support, love, patience and encouragement. They do not need for you to blame them, lecture them or argue with them.

Do you know how discouragement begins? Discouragement begins when reality does not meet with our expectations.

Have you ever really looked forward to doing something special? Maybe there was a special party that you couldn't wait to attend. For weeks you and your friends planned for the "Big Day." Your best friends were coming, the food would be great and the weather was going to be perfect! This would be the party that everyone would remember for the rest of the year.

But now the party's over. As you think about it, the party wasn't as great as you had hoped it would be. Matter of fact, it was just like other parties that you had been to. Now you have become discouraged. The reality (what the party was really like) was not as you had hoped (your expectations).

EXPECTATIONS ≠ REALITY ⟶ DISCOURAGEMENT

Discouragement happens all of the time. That's why the Bible constantly reminds Christians that they have a responsibility to encourage others. "Bear one another's burdens, and so fulfill the law of Christ" (Galatians 6:2).

The word "encourage" involves a commitment to come alongside and help. When you see someone discouraged, scared or carrying a heavy burden, ask yourself this question: "How can I come alongside and help?"

You can give encouragement through a smile, friendly words, a helping hand or just through listening. The most wonderful part of encouragement is this: Anybody can do it! You don't have to have a certain amount of money. You don't have to be a certain size or a certain age. As Elizabeth Pilenko proved, you can give encouragement at any time and in any place.

Whenever you think of encouragement, think of Barnabas. His name means "son of encouragement." Barnabas came to Jerusalem during the Feast of Pentecost the same year that Jesus was crucified. It was during this time that he became a Christian. As a result, he sold all that he had to support the missionary work of the Apostle Paul.

The Book of Acts gives many examples of encouragement shown by Barnabas. He encouraged strangers that he met along the highway (Acts 14:19–22). He believed in Paul when no one else trusted him (Acts 9:26–27). He took a chance on John Mark when Paul had given up on him (Acts 15:36–41). His whole life could be summarized by the words of Acts 11:22–24:

". . . and they sent out Barnabas to go as far as Antioch. When he came and had seen the grace of God, he was glad, and encouraged them all that with purpose of heart they should continue with the Lord. For he was a good man, full of the Holy Spirit and of faith . . . ."

Do you know anyone like Barnabas? Has there been someone in your life who has encouraged you and been there when you were discouraged?

Who in your life needs a Barnabas right now? Maybe God is challenging you to become a Barnabas. Are there friends, family, neighbors, teachers or others who could use your encouragement today?

Take time to write a note, share a word of encouragement, give an anonymous surprise or a helping hand to show that you care. Let God use you to encourage others' lives today.

INQUIRY-ACTION 24.1

ENCOURAGEMENT

1) Related words: _____

_____

2) What is the "core" of these words? _____

3) What does "encourage" mean? _____

_____

4) What are some Bible synonyms for encouragement? _____

_____

5) Why is it easier for us to be discouraged than encouraged? _____

_____

_____

6) Which would God prefer Christians to be—discouraged or encouraged?

_____

7) Why would encouragement be an important characteristic to develop?

_____

_____

INQUIRY-ACTION 24.2
GOD'S ENCOURAGEMENT TO US

God's care   1 Corinthians 2:12

God's rest   2 Timothy 3:16–17

Strength for daily life   1 Peter 5:7

The Bible for help   Matthew 11:28

The Spirit for help   1 Corinthians 10:13

Power over temptation   Colossians 1:10–11

A life of reward here
  and in the future   2 Timothy 4:7–8

Earthly and
  eternal blessing   John 14:1–3

An assurance of
  resurrection   John 10:10

A home in Heaven   1 Thessalonians 4:16–18

Eternal peace
  and happiness   Malachi 3:10

A Crown of Eternal Life   Revelation 21:3–4

INQUIRY-ACTION 24.2 (CONTINUED)

God's love	Titus 3:4–6
Forgiveness of sin	John 17:3
Freedom from guilt	Psalm 52:8
Salvation	Romans 6:23
A personal relationship with God	John 1:12
Membership in God's family	Hebrews 10:22

The Holy Spirit to guard and guide me	1 Peter 1:5
God-given abilities to serve others	Philippians 4:19
God's protection	John 14:16–17
God's peace	Jeremiah 29:11
God's provision	Ephesians 4:11–13
God's plan	Philippians 4:7

INQUIRY-ACTION 24.3

BARNABAS

Name means: _____

I. Barnabas encouraged others through his finances (Acts 4:32–37).

_____

_____

II. Barnabas encouraged others through friendship (Acts 9:23–28).

_____

_____

III. Barnabas encouraged others through fellowship (Acts 11:22–26).

_____

_____

IV. Barnabas encouraged others in spite of obvious failure (Acts 15:36–39).

_____

_____

INQUIRY-ACTION 24.4

"ONE ANOTHER"

Reference	Command

Reference	Command

Reference	Command

Reference	Command

Reference	Command

INQUIRY-ACTION 24.4 (CONTINUED)

SOME PERSONAL THOUGHTS

1. Something I've learned about encouraging others is _____

_____

_____

_____

_____

2. Something I've learned about myself being encouraged is _____

_____

_____

_____

_____

3. A decision I've made based on this study is _____

_____

_____

_____

_____

4. I can be more encouraging to others by _____

_____

_____

_____

INQUIRY-ACTION 24.5

ENCOURAGING WORDS / ENCOURAGING ACTIONS

Look up each of the following verses and place the verse reference in either the "Encouraging Words" or "Encouraging Actions" column noted below: Proverbs 12:25; Romans 12:15; Proverbs 16:24; Galatians 6:2; Proverbs 18:21; Colossians 3:12.

After looking up each of the verses and placing the words in the appropriate column, give examples of encouraging words and actions in home, church and school.

Encouraging Words	**Encouraging Actions**
Verses:	Verses:
Examples:	Examples:
– at home	– at home
– at church	– at church
– at school	– at school

INQUIRY-ACTION 24.6

2 THESSALONIANS 2:16–17

Select words, add capitals and punctuation to write the verses.

now may our lord jesus christ himself and our god even and our father which who has hath loved us and by his grace hath given us grace everlasting eternal consolation encouragement comfort and good hope by through grace comfort and encourage strengthen your hearts and strengthen establish you in every good work deed word and word work

DISCERNMENT

Knowing the Difference between Truth and Error

It's not always easy to distinguish between what's real and what's fake. The story is told about a young lady (we'll call her Amy) who had just graduated from cooking school. Amy had been hired by one of the finest restaurants in the city and was to begin work the following week.

In celebration of her accomplishments, Amy threw a big party at her home and invited her closest friends. She would show them her cooking abilities by preparing gourmet delicacies for the evening. It was time to put her talents to the ultimate test!

However, this hostess was more than a gourmet chef. Amy also liked to play jokes on her friends. Little did one of her guests know that this would be an evening he would never forget.

As the party got under way, Amy circulated among her guests with a beautiful tray of hors d'oeuvres. But there was something strangely different about some of these hors d'oeuvres. The meat was dog food! The dog food was served on delicate little crackers with a wedge of imported cheese, bacon chips, an olive and a sliver of pimiento on top. These were hors d'oeuvres a la Alpo.

Amy had singled out one of her guests (we'll call him Michael) to be the recipient of her joke that evening. When she offered him the hors d'oeuvres a la Alpo, he quickly gobbled one down. Much to her surprise, he just couldn't get enough of this tasty treat! As the evening went on and Amy explained to all of her other guests what she had done, they all watched in amazement as Michael kept coming back for more. Michael even asked Amy for the recipe!

Eventually, Michael was told that he was eating dog food. Although it wasn't dangerous to his health, can you imagine how he felt when he realized that he had eaten the equivalent of a full can of dog food? This story perfectly illustrates something that happens every day all around us. Religious fakes, professional charlatans, counterfeit Christians—call them whatever you like—"disguise themselves as servants of righteousness" (2 Corinthians 11:13–15 NIV), but are completely phony. The religious group known as Heaven's Gate is a recent example.

On March 26, 1997, 39 bodies were discovered inside a hilltop mansion in Rancho Santa Fe, California. According to law enforcement authorities, these 39 people were cult members who planned their mass suicide, videotaped farewells, packed their suitcases for what they believed would be an intergalactic trip, and then took their own lives by drinking a homemade recipe of drugs, applesauce and vodka.

In one newspaper account, the Heaven's Gate group was described as a combination of New Age spirituality, distorted Christianity, Internet computer technology and space-age science fiction. They believed that by taking their own lives they would "graduate" to a "higher level" that could only be reached through a rendezvous with a UFO trailing behind the Hale-Bopp comet.

While this is certainly a strange and bizarre story, it has a very sad aspect. The cult was the creation of Marshall Applewhite over 20 years ago. During that 20 year period, 38 additional people accepted his beliefs as true. They were so sure he spoke the truth that they willingly took their own lives in preparation for a rendezvous with a UFO!

Just like many other men and women through the centuries, the members of Heaven's Gate lacked discernment. They were unable to tell the difference between truth and falsehood. As a result of following a lie, they took their own lives.

Every week you face important decisions in your life. Some of these decisions relate to school, some to family and friends and some to how you conduct your life. In all of these decisions, there is an important question that you must ask yourself: "Where do I look for guidance when I make my decisions?" When making decisions, we must be able to say that we have chosen "God's Way" over the "World's

Way." There is a big difference between decisions that conform to this world and decisions that honor God. When decisions are made the World's Way, man becomes the center of attention. Whether a decision is right or wrong is the not the question asked. Rather, when decisions are made the World's Way, man asks "What do I want to do?"

Discernment, knowing the difference between truth and falsehood, means the same thing as knowing the difference between God's Way and the World's Way. God's Way is always the truthful and right way. The World's Way is always false, leading to destruction. That is why the Apostle Paul, in Romans 12:1–2, begs us "Do not be conformed to this world, but be transformed by the renewing of your mind, that you may prove what is that good and acceptable and perfect will of God." Another word for "prove" is "discern."

Jesus made a similar point in His parable of the wise man and the foolish man (Matthew 7:24–27). One built his house on the rock, the other on the sand. When the storm came, the foolish man's house collapsed, but the wise man's house on the rock stood firm. The wise man was the one who, Jesus said, "hears these sayings of Mine, and does them."

By choosing God's Way over the World's Way, you are demonstrating the character trait of discernment. If you build your life upon the truth of God's Word, you will never have to worry about making the right decision.

God's Word gives us four steps to follow when we are faced with a decision. If you will follow each of these steps, He will give you discernment as you make the decisions that you face in life.

Step 1:   Determine what God's Word says about the decision you
            need to make.

No matter what decision you face, God's Word will provide principles to guide you. The Psalmist said, "Your word have I hidden in my heart, that I might not sin against You" (Psalm 119:11). God's Word keeps us from making decisions the World's Way.

Step 2:   Pray for God's clear guidance in the decision that you
            need to make.

As you quiet yourself before the Lord in prayer, He will direct your path. In 1 Thessalonians 5:17, we are told to "pray without ceasing." Praying without ceasing does not mean that we spend our entire lives on our knees. Prayer is not a position before God; it is a relationship with God. To "pray without ceasing" means to constantly seek God in all of the issues we face in life. It is a willingness to listen to Him at all times.

Step 3:   Talk with someone, with whom you have confidence, about the decision you need to make.

In Proverbs 15:22 (NIV) we are told that "in the multitude of counselors there is wisdom." This is God's advice to us to talk over our decision with others. Remember, however, that God wants us to seek counselors who are godly people. God's wisdom does not come from those who do not know Him or love Him.

Step 4:   Realize that God will "open" and "close" doors related to the decision that you need to make.

Too often when Christians pray for God's help to make a decision, they have already made up their minds as to what God's decision should be. When we do that, we are not being honest with God. Actually, what we are doing is asking God to agree with the decision we have already made. When we "run ahead of God," we are making decisions the World's Way.

When making decisions, God requires that we trust Him (Proverbs 3:5) and that we wait patiently on Him (James 1:3). As we approach each step of the decision, God will open the way (His way) for us to take the next step. As we step through the open door, God's Way will become clear.

Without godly discernment, you will not be able to tell the difference between what is true and what is false. That doesn't necessarily mean that you will eat dog food hors d'oeuvres or rendezvous with a UFO. But it does mean that decisions in your life will be made according to the World's Way.

God's Way is always best. He will give you the discernment to make the right decisions if you will put Him first in your life.

INQUIRY-ACTION 25.1

DISCERNING TRUTH

Some truths about God:

Some truths about Christ:

Some truths about God's Word:

INQUIRY-ACTION 25.1 (CONTINUED)

Some truths about me and my relationship with God:

Some actions I need to take based on these truths:

INQUIRY-ACTION 25.2

You shall know the truth, and the truth shall make you free (John 8:38).

Free from . . .

_____   _____

_____   _____

_____   _____

_____   _____

_____   _____

_____   _____

_____   _____

_____   _____

INQUIRY-ACTION 25.3

CHOOSING GOD'S WAY
OR
CHOOSING THE WORLD'S WAY

Identify one characteristic of godly decision-making and worldly decision-making. Write it under the appropriate column. When your classmates share their responses, add them to your list.

Characteristics of godly decision-making:	Characteristics of worldly decision-making:
1.	1.
2.	2.
3.	3.
4.	4.
5.	5.
6.	6.
7.	7.

INQUIRY-ACTION 25.4

Step One:

Determine what God's Word says about the decision you need to make.

My Response

_____

_____

Step Two:

Pray for God's clear guidance in the decision that you need to make.

My Response

_____

_____

INQUIRY–ACTION 25.4 (CONTINUED)

Step Three:

Talk with someone, with whom you have confidence, about the decision you need to make.

My Response

_____
_____
_____

Step Four:

Realize that God will "open and close doors" related to the decision that you need to make.

My Response

_____
_____
_____

INQUIRY-ACTION 25.5

WHAT ADVICE HAVE YOU RECEIVED?

Every day someone gives you advice. List the "good" and "bad" advice you have received recently. Then record the consequences of taking that advice.

Good Advice:	Bad Advice:	Consequences:
1.	1.	1.
2.	2.	2.
3.	3.	3.
4.	4.	4.
5	5.	5.

INQUIRY-ACTION 25.6

PHILIPPIANS 1:9–10

Place the letters so that the words and phrases for the verses are in sequence. Not all phrases will be used.

_____

_____

_____

(a) yet

(b) until

(c) more and more

(d) you may

(e) I pray

(f) approve

(g) depth of insight

(h) the day of Christ

(i) your love

(j) are excellent

(k) in real knowledge

(l) till

(m) And this

(n) be able to discern

(o) in all judgment

(p) all discernment

(q) may be

(r) may abound

(s) things

(t) the things

(u) and

(v) without offense

(w) in order to

(x) and blameless

(y) that

(z) in knowledge

(aa) is my prayer

(bb) what is best

(cc) still

(dd) be sincere

(ee) that ye may

(ff) so that

(gg) pure

SINCERITY

Being Genuine in All You Say and Do

There are a number of phrases, spoken by famous individuals, that have become well known over the years. General Douglas A. MacArthur told the Filipino people, as he was forced from the Philippines during World War II, "I shall return!" President Harry S Truman reminded the American people that he personally took the final responsibility for decisions made by the government when he said, "The buck stops here!" Civil Rights leader Martin Luther King, Jr., challenged a nation to put aside racial differences when he said, "I have a dream!"

In 1872 the American journalist Henry M. Stanley gave a simple greeting that would be recorded in the pages of history forever. The following story is not only about the famous words of that greeting, but also about a man who was known for his sincerity.

Henry Stanley, a journalist with the *New York World*, had been sent to Africa by the paper's editor to find the noted medical missionary, David Livingstone. It was reported that Livingstone had been murdered by one of the local tribes. Stanley's task was to find Livingstone or his remains and come back with a story.

Born in England, David Livingstone studied both medicine and theology in the early 1830's. Dr. Livingstone knew that God had called him to be more than just a medical doctor. He knew that God was calling him to evangelism. However, his call was not to evangelize England, or even Europe. God had called him to the great continent of Africa.

In 1841 Dr. Livingstone arrived at one of the many African mission stations. Although he faithfully served the Lord there for a number of years, Dr. Livingstone knew that God expected more from him.

Over the next 15 years, Dr. Livingstone felt God's call to the difficult task of opening the interior of Africa to the Gospel. Many of his friends tried to convince him that if he ventured into the heart of the African continent, he would never be heard from again. However, it was Dr. Livingstone's conviction that there were hundreds of African tribes that had never heard the Gospel of Jesus Christ. He believed that it was his responsibility to not only care for them physically, but also spiritually.

The missionary made his last visit to England in 1865; when he returned to Africa the next year, he vanished into the interior. He was not seen or heard from for the next five years, giving rise to the rumors that sent journalist Henry Stanley on his quest in 1871.

Stanley and his party searched for Livingstone for nearly a year. As he went from village to village, he would learn that Dr. Livingstone had been there and then moved to another village.

Late one afternoon Stanley learned that an elderly white man had entered the village of Ujiji. Stanley set out immediately for the village, arriving there in a few days. When he pushed through the crowds, he saw the man he had been seeking for months. Describing their meeting, Stanley wrote in his journal:

> *I . . . would have embraced him, only, he being an*
> *Englishman, I did not know how he would receive me:*
> *so I did what moral cowardice and false pride suggested*
> *was the best thing—I walked deliberately to him, took*
> *off my hat and said: "Dr. Livingstone, I presume?"*

"Dr. Livingstone, I presume?" is a phrase that brings to mind visions of Africa whenever it is spoken. These words also remind us of the sincerity of one of God's choice servants—Dr. David Livingstone.

Dr. Livingstone knew that God had saved him from his sins and had given him the ability to become a doctor. He also knew that it is the responsibility of all believers to evangelize the world and that Africa was a nation in need of both the Gospel and medical help. Because it was his sincere desire to obey his Heavenly Father, he knew that he must use the talents God had given him to reach the tribes of Africa.

As Christians, we have a responsibility to be sincere both in what we say and what we do. We must be willing to "walk the walk" and "talk the talk," no matter who we are with or in what circumstances we find ourselves. If we profess Jesus Christ as our personal Savior, our words and deeds must be consistent with His teachings. In the Sermon on the Mount (Matthew 5:1–16) Jesus provided one of the clearest explanations of what it means to live a sincere life.

The Sermon on the Mount was the first, and longest, message spoken during Jesus' teaching ministry. Many scholars believe that it was given during the first year of His public ministry. Christians have interpreted the Sermon on the Mount in various ways. Some view the sermon as the Lord's statement of the way of salvation. Others view it as Jesus' teaching about the "end times."

All scholars agree that the sermon provides the Lord's clearest teaching about how mankind should relate to one another, as well as to God. It is in the Sermon on the Mount that some of the most famous statements of Jesus are recorded, including: the Beatitudes, the call to love our enemies and the Lord's Prayer.

In the Sermon on the Mount, the Lord teaches us eight lessons about sincerity. Note how each of the following lessons requires us to be "genuine" in our relationships with God and others. In His sermon, the Lord reminds us that we should be sincere. . .

> . . . in our understanding that we are sinners, redeemed by God (verse 3)
> . . . in our compassion for others (verse 4)
> . . . in our humility before God and others (verse 5)
> . . . in our desire to know God (verse 6)
> . . . in our willingness to forgive others (verse 7)
> . . . in our desire to live righteously (verse 8)
> . . . in our peaceful relationships with others (verse 9)
> . . . in our consistent life before all men (verse 10)

In which of these areas do you lack sincerity? Do you have compassion, or ridicule, for your fellow students? Is it your desire to know more about God, or more about the latest gossip in the weekly tabloid? Do you seek to maintain peaceful relationships with those in your school, or do you look for ways to "put them down" and cause them anger and hurt?

If you claim to be a Christian, then sincerity must characterize your life. Dr. Livingstone realized that his words and actions had to be a genuine response to what he believed. As a result, he devoted his life to the continent of Africa.

God may not be calling you to Africa, but He is calling you to be genuine in all that you say and do. He is calling you to be sincere in your relationship to Him and to others.

INQUIRY-ACTION 26.1

SINCERITY	VS.	HYPOCRISY
Basic Meaning		
Descriptions of People		
Lesson to Be Learned		

INQUIRY-ACTION 26.2

How Others See Me

_____

_____

_____

_____

_____

_____

_____

_____

_____

_____

_____

James 1:21–22 _____

_____

_____

INQUIRY-ACTION 26.2 (CONTINUED)

How God Sees Me

_____

_____

_____

_____

_____

_____

_____

_____

_____

_____

_____

1 Samuel 16:7 _____

_____

_____

INQUIRY-ACTION 26.2 (CONTINUED)

How I Want to Be Seen by God and Others

_____

_____

_____

_____

_____

_____

_____

_____

_____

_____

Philippians 4:8 _____

_____

INQUIRY-ACTION 26.3

SINCERITY ACTION PLAN

1. The difference between how others see me and how I would like others to see me:

_____

_____

_____

_____

2. The difference between how God sees me and how I want God to see me:

_____

_____

_____

_____

Inquiry-Action 26.3 (CONTINUED)

3. I can take the following steps to become more sincere in my relationships with God and with others. In other words, I must take the following steps to remove the differences between how God and others view me and how I want to be viewed by God and others.

_____

_____

_____

_____

_____

_____

_____

_____

_____

_____

INQUIRY-ACTION 26.4

INTERVIEW RECORD — SINCERITY

Definition:

_____

_____

Importance:

_____

_____

_____

_____

Scriptural Example:

_____

_____

_____

Everyday Example:

_____

_____

_____

INQUIRY-ACTION 26.4 (CONTINUED)

Evidences of Sincerity:

_____

_____

_____

Evidences of Hypocrisy:

_____

_____

_____

Attitude toward Hypocrisy:

_____

_____

_____

Ways to Best Avoid Hypocrisy:

_____

_____

_____

Ways to Best Develop Sincerity:

_____

_____

_____

INQUIRY-ACTION 26.5

1 PETER 1:22–23

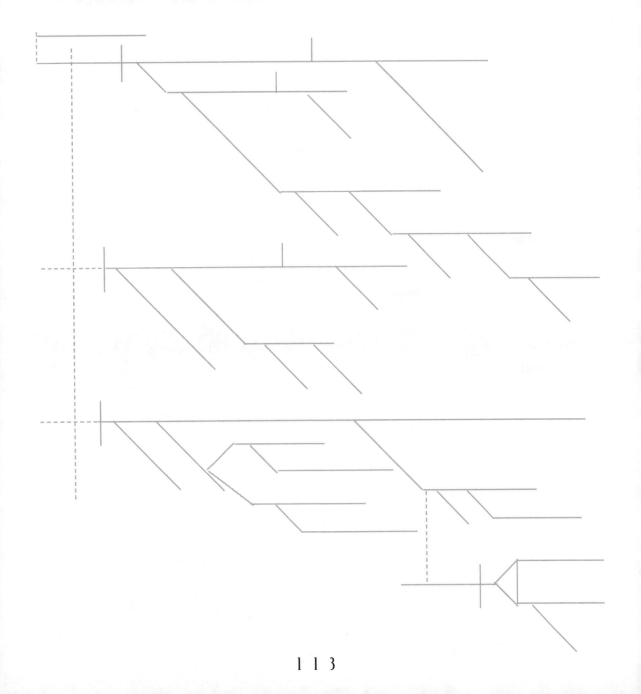

INQUIRY-ACTION 26.5 (CONTINUED)

1 PETER 2:1–2

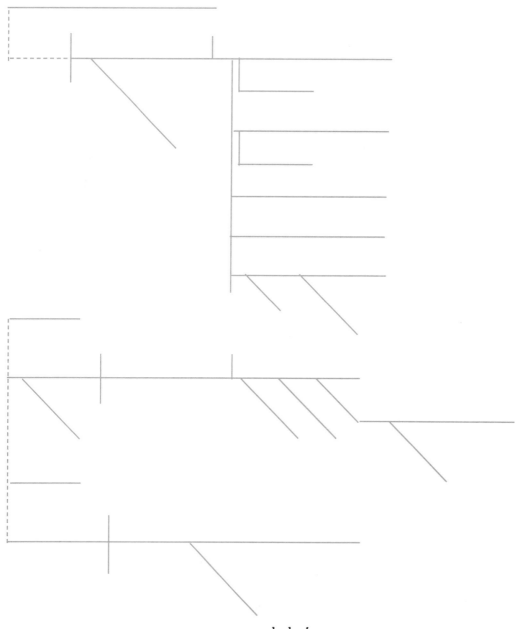

PURITY

The Moral Standard for All Believers

Do you like the comics in the Sunday paper? All across the country, every weekend, millions of readers enjoy their imaginary friends. Although these people wouldn't be "caught dead" watching Saturday morning cartoons, they eagerly catch up on *Garfield*, *Hi and Lois* or *Beetle Bailey*.

One of the more popular comics portrays a caveman named B.C. One day B.C. was leaning on his famous boulder. The rock is inscribed "Trivia Test," and B.C. is administering the exam to one of his prehistoric buddies.

"Here's one from the Bible," he says. "What were the last words uttered by Lot's wife?"

Without a moment's hesitation, B.C.'s friend replied, "I don't care what you think, I'm going to take one last look!"

The Bible does not tell us what Lot's wife actually said as he and his family fled from the city of Sodom. But the Bible does tell us what God said: "Escape for your life! Do not look behind you nor stay anywhere in the plain. Escape to the mountains, lest you be destroyed" (Genesis 19:17).

The wickedness in the city of Sodom would have exceeded any of today's major cities. According to Genesis 18 and 19, the city was filled with people who practiced all types of perversions. Because of the terrible sin of this city, God punished the city with the worst holocaust in the history of ancient civilization. "Then the Lord rained brimstone and fire on Sodom and Gomorrah from the Lord out of the heavens. So He overthrew those cities, all the plain, all the inhabitants of the cities, and what grew on the ground" (Genesis 19:24–26).

As Sodom and Gomorrah were being destroyed from the face of the earth, Lot and his family were running for their lives. While the corrupt cities sank slowly into the waters of the Dead Sea, it looked as if Lot's family had escaped the destruction. That is, everyone but Lot's wife. We don't know if she told her husband what she was going to do, but she did look back. Apparently she couldn't bring herself to believe that God meant what He said.

It is interesting how the Bible records her death: "But his wife looked back behind him, and she became a pillar of salt" (Genesis 19:26).

Mrs. Lot refused to cut off her emotional ties to these sinful cities. To quote the caveman's friend, "I don't care what you think, I'm going to take one last look." It is quite possible that on Mrs. Lot's tombstone you might find the following words:

THERE IS NO NEED TO TAKE GOD SERIOUSLY!

This is certainly the philosophy that is popular today. Just as Mrs. Lot was unable to leave the sinful city of Sodom behind her, there are many others today who are unable to put the sins of an impure lifestyle behind them. They do not take seriously Biblical warnings such as 1 Thessalonians 4:7: ". . . for God did not call us to uncleanness, but to holiness."

Joseph certainly understood the importance of maintaining a pure life. In Genesis 39 it is recorded that as a result of God's blessing, Joseph had become overseer of Potiphar's house. Because Potiphar was an officer of Pharaoh, Joseph had a powerful position.

It was not long before Joseph became acquainted with Potiphar's wife. Beginning with verse 7, the Bible tells the story of how Potiphar's wife tried to get Joseph to go to bed with her. Joseph repeatedly refused, but Potiphar's wife continued to pursue him. Finally, Joseph had to flee from Potiphar's home in order to remove himself from the temptation and remain pure.

Unlike Lot's wife, Joseph did not look back. He did not want any part of the wickedness Potiphar's wife was proposing. Because of Joseph's devotion to God, he was able to maintain a pure mind and pure thoughts. Because his mind and thoughts were pure, he was able to remain pure in his actions.

There is an important principle to be learned from the life of Joseph: PURE THOUGHTS = PURE ACTIONS. Because Joseph's mind was focused on God, his actions reflected God's righteousness.

The mind is the key to maintaining purity. That is why God instructed the Apostle Paul to write the following: "And do not be conformed to this world, but be transformed by the renewing of your mind . . ." (Romans 12:2a). If we allow the world to squeeze us into its mold and fill our minds with worldly thoughts, then we will behave like the world. If our minds are filled with God's truth, then we will behave in a righteous manner.

Throughout His entire ministry, the Lord Jesus Christ was busy healing the sick (Matthew 9:12; Luke 4:23). This was such a regular part of His work that the Lord has been frequently referred to as the Great Physician. He was capable of healing anyone—even raising people from the dead.

Suppose the Great Physician were to look at your life. What types of impure behaviors would He see? Are you a patient who is suffering from sexual immorality? lying? stealing? cheating? profanity? fighting?

If the Great Physician were to take an even closer look into your mind, what would He see? Would He see thoughts that are pure or impure? Would your mind be filled with the lyrics from the latest rock song, or caught up in watching *The Simpsons* or reading the new edition of the *Sports Illustrated* swimsuit issue? Remember, the purity of your thoughts affects the purity of your actions.

The world constantly bombards us with a perspective that ignores God. If we are not careful, it's easy to lose our heavenly perspective. Renewing your mind involves getting rid of wrong, worldly thinking and developing a "Word-ly" perspective. Consider the following verses from Psalm 119:

"Your word I have hidden in my heart, that I might not sin against You" (verse 11).

"Turn my eyes away from looking at worthless things, and revive me in Your way" (verse 37).

"Oh, how I love Your law! It is my meditation all the day" (verse 97).

"I opened my mouth and panted, for I longed for Your commandments" (verse 131).

How healthy would you be if you ate junk food all the time? If you avoid food that is healthy, it will not be long before you become sick and lose your strength.

The same is true with your mind. It's no wonder that so many Christians are "sick" in the head. They fill their minds with the world's over-sexed, profane junk and seldom take in the truth of God's Word.

In order to prevent, or cure, a sick mind, the Great Physician recommends His Word as the only medication. It should be taken as follows:

1) **Read it.** Don't rely on learning isolated verses. Read chapters at a time.

2) **Study it.** Seriously seek to understand what God's Word is saying to you.

3) **Memorize it.** Hide God's Word in your heart. This gives you the ammo needed to fight temptation and discouragement.

4) **Meditate on it.** Thinking on the meaning of Scripture brings us closer to God and helps give us His perspective on the world.

Remember: PURE THOUGHTS = PURE ACTIONS. The mind is the key to a pure life. When temptations come, run from them! Don't look back. Take God seriously, for He means what He says. "Remember Lot's wife!" (Luke 17:32).

INQUIRY-ACTION 27.1

TEXT SUMMARY

1. Describe God's judgment on a Bible person of impurity.

_____

_____

2. Describe God's blessing on a Bible person of purity.

_____

_____

3. Describe how God works through His Word to produce purity in our lives.

_____

_____

4. How should we treat God's Word? What should we do with it?

_____

_____

5. If Jesus, the Great Physician, were to X-ray your heart and mind, what kind of surgery would be required? (You can answer on another sheet of paper if desired. Your words should be for Jesus alone.)

_____

_____

INQUIRY-ACTION 27.2

PURITY CHECKLIST

If I want to know whether a thought or action is pure, I should think . . .

1.

2.

INQUIRY-ACTION 27.2 (CONTINUED)

3.

4.

5.

INQUIRY–ACTION 27.3

PURITY CHECKLIST

If I want to know whether a thought or action is pure, I should think . . .

Checkpoint 1:

_____

_____

_____

Checkpoint 2:

_____

_____

_____

Checkpoint 3:

_____

_____

_____

INQUIRY-ACTION 27.3 (CONTINUED)

Checkpoint 4:

_____

_____

_____

_____

Checkpoint 5:

_____

_____

_____

_____

Checkpoint 6:

_____

_____

_____

_____

Checkpoint 7:

_____

_____

_____

_____

INQUIRY–ACTION 27.4

Based on the lessons this week related to purity, I want to make the following commitments to myself and God.

1. _____

   _____

   _____

2. _____

   _____

   _____

3. _____

   _____

   _____

_____

Signature

_____

Date

INQUIRY-ACTION 27.5

1 CORINTHIANS 6:19–20

Or _____ you _____ know _____ your _____ is _____ temple _____ the

_____ Spirit _____ is _____ you, _____ you _____ from _____,

and _____ are _____ your _____ ? For _____ were _____ at _____

price; _____ glorify _____ in _____ body _____ in

_____ spirit, _____ are _____'s.

Or _____ _____ not _____ _____ your _____ _____ the

_____ _____ _____ the _____ _____ who _____ _____ you,

_____ _____ have _____ _____, and _____ _____ not

_____ _____ ? For _____ _____ bought _____ _____ price;

_____ God _____ _____ body _____

_____ your _____, _____ are _____'s.

Or _____ _____ _____ know _____ _____ _____ _____ _____

_____ of _____ _____ _____ who _____ _____ _____,

whom _____ _____ _____ God, and _____ _____ _____ your

_____ ? _____ _____ were _____ _____ _____ price;

_____ _____ _____ in _____ _____

_____ in _____ _____, _____ are _____'s.

INQUIRY–ACTION 27.5 (CONTINUED)

Or _____ _____ _____ _____ that _____ _____ _____

_____ temple _____ _____ _____ _____ who _____

_____ _____ , _____ you _____ _____ _____ , _____

you _____ _____ _____ _____ ? For _____ _____

_____ _____ a _____ ; _____ _____ _____

_____ _____ in _____ _____ _____ _____

your _____ , _____ _____ _____ ' __ .

_____

_____

_____

_____

_____

_____

MATURITY

Responding and Behaving as Jesus Would

The headlines on the Feature Page were clear: "Airlines Say More Passengers Unruly." Under the photograph accompanying the article were these words: "Airline authorities respond quickly, including handcuffs, to violence that threatens their crews." It seems that the "friendly skies" are not as friendly as they used to be. The story behind the headlines is as follows:

> On a crowded flight from Chicago to Las Vegas, an America West airlines flight attendant was pushed to the floor by a female passenger who became angry when told there were no extra sandwiches. Although the passenger was sentenced to two years probation and 200 hours of community service, the flight attendant still has nightmares about the incident.

> "It's gotten so you're almost afraid to ask passengers to raise their seat backs, or put up their tray tables, for fear of what might happen," the flight attendant said.

This is not an isolated incident. Airlines have reported a surge of disruptive behaviors in recent months. Passengers regularly curse or spit on flight attendants, throw food trays in anger and have even attacked pilots walking down the aisle.

But this type of behavior is not limited to airplanes. It is continued in the baggage claim area and at the car rental counters. Passengers have been known to explode in rage over delayed flights, unavailable rental cars or missing luggage. "Airline passengers mirror society," said one spokeswoman for the Association of Flight Attendants. "They're less willing to accept problems or delays, and many of them are aggressive, like so many drivers."

You have probably seen this kind of rude, explosive behavior in everyday experiences—riding in the car, attending a sports event, waiting in line at a store. More and more, people openly show immature responses of anger and frustration when they don't get their way.

Have you ever been in a situation where you were embarrassed by the actions of a family member or another person? Did you note how "out of control" these people were when they responded? They were certainly not responding in a Christian manner. Responding and behaving Christ-like is a sign of maturity—the subject of this week's lesson and one of the most important character traits you will study this semester.

If you are like most students your age, you are looking forward to "growing up." Have you ever stopped to think about what growing up (becoming mature) really means? Although growing taller and getting older are signs of maturity, there is more to becoming mature than physical changes.

You have probably already entered that well-known period of life called "adolescence." If you were to ask most people what it means to be an adolescent, they would probably reply, "a teenager." In the minds of most people, an adolescent is someone between the ages of 13 and 19.

But the period of adolescence is not just the teenage years. The word "adolescence" comes from a Latin term, "adolescere," which means "to grow to maturity." Adolescence is not a period of time (for example, the teenage years); it is a process of maturing. It is that time of life when you begin to talk and act less like a child and more like an adult.

For some young people, adolescence begins before they enter their teenage years. For others, the process of adolescence extends beyond the teenage years. However long it may take, God has a unique time period set aside for that transition to take place in your life.

Since adolescence is a time when you "grow to maturity," what does it mean to be mature? Maturity is the process of growth that includes four distinct areas: physical, mental, social and spiritual. Developing properly in each of these areas contributes toward your becoming a mature individual.

You have probably already noticed the physical changes that are taking place in your life—rapid growth, change in voice, etc. These are changes over which you have little control, but which indicate that you are on the path to maturity. Although these physical changes are not under your control, you do have an important responsibility while they are taking place. You must take care of your physical body during this time in your life. Eating properly and getting enough sleep and exercise are essential to helping your body grow to maturity. The Apostle Paul challenges us to take care of our physical bodies when he says, ". . . present your bodies a living sacrifice, holy, acceptable to God, which is your reasonable service" (Romans 12:1).

There are also mental changes taking place in your life. You are beginning to think about things in a very different way. For example, you are starting to realize how what you say affects others and what they think of you. Words can have meanings beyond their definitions. You have to take responsibility for what you say. Do you find yourself thinking more about your future? That is also a part of the mental change taking place in your life. You are no longer thinking as a child but have begun to think like an adult. Notice what Paul says in 1Corinthians 13:11, "When I was a child, I spoke as a child, I understood as a child, I thought as a child; but when I became a man, I put away childish things."

Other than physical, probably the greatest area of change you are noticing right now is in the area of your social relationships. When boys and girls are little, they often play by themselves and seldom like to be seen with members of the opposite sex. Now that you are starting to mature, you find yourself wanting to have a number of friends, including those of the opposite sex. You have probably also become very concerned about the way you look, talk and relate to others. This is all a natural part of the social changes taking place as you "grow to maturity."

The Bible has a lot to say about our relationships with others. In Ephesians 4 the Apostle Paul says the following about how we talk and act around others:

> "speak the truth in love" (verse 15)
> "put off. . .deceitful lusts" (verse 22)
> "be renewed in the spirit of your mind" (verse 23)
> "let no corrupt word proceed out of your mouth" (verse 29)
> "do not grieve the Holy Spirit of God" (verse 30)
> "be kind to one another" (verse 32)

During this period of your life, you are also experiencing some of the greatest spiritual changes you have ever faced. Research has shown that it is during adolescence that most young people either commit totally to God or turn away from God. Many Christian leaders trace their decisions for full-time service to God back to their early adolescence. These are wonderful years for sincere commitments to the Lord.

Remember, God does not wait until you "grow to maturity" to use you in His service. When Daniel refused to bow down to Nebuchadnezzar's golden image and was cast into the fiery furnace (Daniel 3), he was an adolescent. When David fought and killed Goliath (1 Samuel 17), he was still an adolescent. Scholars believe that when Mary ". . . was found with child of the Holy Spirit" (Matthew 1:18), she was an adolescent. Throughout the Bible, and history in general, God has mightily used adolescents.

This week's key verse puts into perspective the spiritual challenge that you face as you grow to maturity: "That we should no longer be children. . .but. . .may grow up in all things into him who is the head—Christ" (Ephesians 4:14a, 15).

Consider your words and actions from the last 24 hours. Did you demonstrate rudeness and immature behavior with any of your friends, teachers or family? If it is your desire to grow to maturity, determine that from now on "responding and behaving as Jesus would" will become the focus of your life.

Inquiry-Action 28.1

Parent Questionnaire

Ask your parents to complete the two statements below. You can record their answers or ask them to write their answers.

The most <u>immature</u> thing I see junior highers doing is . . .

MOM: _____

_____

_____

_____

DAD: _____

_____

_____

_____

INQUIRY-ACTION 28.1 (CONTINUED)

Ask your parents to complete the two statements below. You can record their answers or ask them to write their answers.

The most <u>mature</u> thing I see junior highers doing is . . .

MOM: _____

_____

_____

_____

DAD: _____

_____

_____

_____

INQUIRY-ACTION 28.2

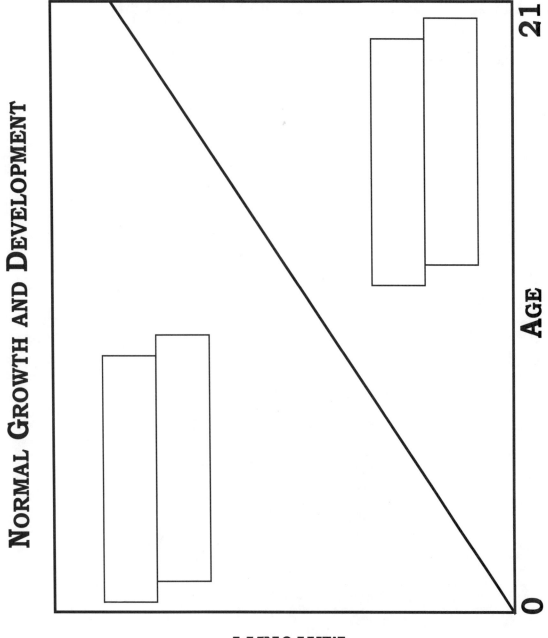

NORMAL GROWTH AND DEVELOPMENT

MATURITY

AGE

0

21

INQUIRY-ACTION 28.3

MATURITY IS SHOWN IN MY CHOICES!

1. Advance Decision Making: _____

_____

_____

_____

_____

_____

2. Delayed Gratification: _____

_____

_____

_____

_____

_____

INQUIRY-ACTION 28.3 (CONTINUED)

3. Consistency: _____

_____

_____

_____

_____

4. Handling Problems: _____

_____

_____

_____

_____

5. Putting Others First: _____

_____

_____

_____

_____

INQUIRY-ACTION 28.4

DECISIONS/ACTIONS

Make a list of the typical decisions and actions made by students each day. Don't limit your decisions and actions only at school.

1. getting up on time

2. dressing for school

3. keeping my room or locker

4. arriving at class

5. being a student

6. being a team member

7. participating in hobbies or personal activities

8. using free time

9. interacting with friends

10. eating

11. interacting with family

12. completing homework

13. personal hygiene

14. going to sleep

15. caring for siblings

16. _____

17. _____

18. _____

19. _____

20. _____

_____

INQUIRY-ACTION 28.4 (CONTINUED)

SHOWING MATURE BEHAVIOR

1. _____

_____

_____

2. _____

_____

_____

3. _____

_____

_____

4. _____

_____

_____

5. _____

_____

_____

6. _____

_____

_____

INQUIRY-ACTION 28.5

EPHESIANS 4:14A AND 15

Draw a line from word to word without crossing more than one line or corner between words. Write the verse at the bottom.

no	more	children	that	is	even	Then
back	Him	unto	is	head	Christ	That
and	things	all	which	the	is	we
forth	henceforth	all	Then	things	who	which
Christ	be	we	That	all	Him	things
head	no	should	will	in	into	all
more	longer	no	are	in	up	in
children	be	infants	all	things	grow	will
tossed	children	tossed	forth	in	may	we
love	to	back	fro	we	will	love
the	here	and	there	but	love	in
and	there	forth	instead	speaking	the	truth

CONTROLLED SPEECH

Honoring God and Others through Your Words

Did you know that Abraham Lincoln's coffin has been pried open twice?

The first time it happened was in 1887, 22 years after Lincoln was assassinated. If you are wondering why, it wasn't for a logical reason. It was not to determine if Lincoln had died of a bullet fired from John Wilkes Booth's derringer. It happened because of a rumor. All across the country a rumor was spreading that Lincoln's coffin was empty. In order to disprove the rumor, the casket was exhumed and opened to reveal the remains of Lincoln's body.

The second time it happened was 14 years later. Although you may find it hard to believe, the same rumor surfaced again. There were loud shouts of protest from those who knew that this was just a rumor. However, the rumor persisted and the pressure mounted to such proportions that the casket was once again lifted from the ground and the lid pried open. Of course, Lincoln's body was still in his coffin.

Officials felt the rumors should be laid to rest along with the Civil War President. Finally, his body was permanently placed in a crypt at Springfield, Illinois.

Think about how hard it was on Lincoln's family to listen to the rumors, accusations and speculation. Then they had to relive the horrible memories of the past as the coffin was removed from the ground and opened—not once, but twice!

But rumors are like that. Lacking real facts, information is repeated that creates unrest and harm. It is spread by people who get satisfaction from being the center of attention and making themselves look better than someone else.

Great harm can be caused by false and hurtful words. It is for this reason that the Bible contains so many warnings about the tongue. God knows that the words we say can build people up or tear them down. Our words can testify to someone's good reputation or destroy it. The words we speak can be true or filled with lies. Only by controlling our speech can we honor God.

Have you ever stopped to think about your tongue? Not a pretty thought, is it? To the physician it's merely a two-ounce slab of mucous membrane enclosing a complex array of muscles and nerves. Not much to look at but absolutely essential to our everyday lives. Without the tongue, we could not chew, taste, swallow, talk or sing. We could not keep suckers in our mouths or blow trumpets. Without the tongue, our entire world would be reduced to unintelligible grunts.

But the tongue is as dangerous as it is important. James warned: "And the tongue is a fire. . .an unruly evil, full of deadly poison" (James 3:6, 8). Words are like bullets fired from a gun. Once released, they cannot be retrieved. Speech that is not controlled can destroy everything in its path.

Rumors are not the only type of dangerous, uncontrolled speech. Profanity, racial slurs, dirty jokes, boasting and lying are also destructive. The words of Ephesians 4:29 make our responsibility very clear: "Let no corrupt word proceed out of your mouth, but what is good for necessary edification, that it may impart grace to the hearers."

Think about what you hear at school. Would you characterize your speech, and that of your friends, as controlled or uncontrolled? Does it build up or tear down? Let's explore some of the "speech problems" common in junior high school.

Profanity, or swearing, is probably right at the top of the list. Profanity has become so common in our society that even Christians sometimes start using those same words or their slang forms without thinking. If you feel, "What's the big deal?," consider what God says:

"But I say to you that for every idle word men may speak, they will give account of it in the day of judgment" (Matthew 12:36).

"You shall not take the name of the Lord your God in vain, for the Lord will not hold him guiltless who takes His name in vain" (Exodus 20:7).

Not only is profanity a sin against God, it is a terrible reflection on you as a person. One day a salesman walked into the office of a very successful businessman. Before he could even sit down, he noticed a well-positioned sign on the man's desk. It was placed in such a way that all his visitors could not miss it. The words on the sign read: "Swearing is the strongest possible expression of a weak mind!" This successful businessman was sending a clear message to his guests: Swearing is unacceptable and does not impress me.

Lying is probably also on the top ten list of uncontrolled speech problems at your school. No one has to teach us to lie. It comes naturally when we feel guilty, surprised, embarrassed, angry or defensive.

In the Garden of Eden, Satan appeared as a serpent. Using that disguise, he tricked Adam and Eve into turning away from God. That's why Jesus referred to the Devil as "the father of lies" (John 8:44). Ever since that time, the serpent has become a symbol for deception (Matthew 3:7). Like a serpent's poisonous bite, a lying tongue causes spiritual illness.

Have you lied to someone lately? You may be thinking, "Well, it was really only a little white lie." But God demands honesty. "The Lord detests lying lips, but he delights in men who are truthful" (Proverbs 12:22 NIV).

Dirty jokes and racial slurs are becoming increasingly common among Christians. Maybe you don't tell dirty jokes, but if you listen and laugh at them you are just as guilty as if you had told them yourself. Once again, the Bible is very clear: " . . . neither filthiness, nor foolish talking, nor coarse jesting, which are not fitting, but rather giving of thanks" (Ephesians 5:4).

How do you feel when others let you know how rich or wonderful or good-looking or popular they are? Boasting, also called bragging, does not impress people. As a matter of fact, it is a big turn-off in the eyes of others. Bragging is like a big neon light that flashes, "Insecure . . . Insecure . . . Insecure . . . ."

People brag because they believe that who they are is not as important to others as what they own, where they've been, who they know, etc. Remember, in God's eyes you already are special. You don't need to talk about yourself. Listen to the words of Proverbs 27:2: "Let another man praise you, and not your own mouth; a stranger, and not your own lips."

Just as termites can slowly but surely ruin a building from the inside, so the tongue (through gossip, profanity, dirty language, lying and boasting) can gradually destroy you. Imagine throwing a handful of confetti into the air on a windy day and then trying to recover it all a week later. That's how impossible it is to recover the words you have spoken. Once words leave your mouth, they can never be fully taken back.

The next time you start to speak, stop and think first. Consider what you are going to say and how you are going to say it. Remember, words are powerful. The rumors surrounding Abraham Lincoln's empty coffin began with one person. As a result, suspicion and hurt continued for more than 30 years. Be sure that the next words you speak are truthful, encouraging and bring healing to the lives of others.

INQUIRY-ACTION 29.1

THE POWER OF WORDS

The Power of Words to Hurt:

Proverbs 16:28:

_____

Proverbs 18:8:

_____

Proverbs 25:18:

_____

Colossians 3:8:

_____

James 3:14:

_____

The Power of Words to Help:

Romans 14:19:

_____

Ephesians 5:4:

_____

1 Peter 4:11:

_____

James 3:17:

_____

Proverbs 15:1, 4:

_____

INQUIRY–ACTION 29.2

IMPORTANT POINTS TO REMEMBER

1 Gossip

2 Profanity

3 Lying

Inquiry-Action 29.2   (CONTINUED)

4 **Boasting**

5 **Negative Comments**

6 **Coarse Talk**

INQUIRY-ACTION 29.3

GOOD COMMUNICATION

Good _____ requires controlled _____,

as well as controlled _____!

Purposes: Controlled listening helps us . . .

1. _____ information accurately.

2. build _____ by understanding others' points of view and feelings.

3. _____ conflicts.

Principles for Resolving Conflicts:

1. Pay _____.

2. Keep _____ in check.

3. Provide _____ to the person on what was heard.

4. Let that person _____ what you said.

5. Ask _____.

6. Conclude the _____ and commit to the relationship.

INQUIRY-ACTION 29.4

RULES FOR CONTROLLED SPEECH

1) Is it true? _____

_____

_____

_____

2) Is it kind? _____

_____

_____

_____

3) Is it needful? _____

_____

_____

_____

INQUIRY-ACTION 29.4 (CONTINUED)

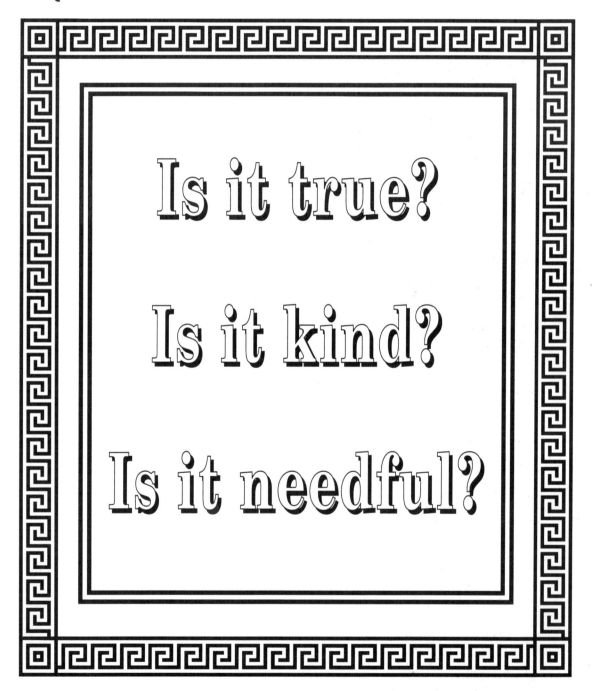

Is it true?

Is it kind?

Is it needful?

INQUIRY-ACTION 29.5

EPHESIANS 4:29, 31–32

L___ n__ c____ ___ ___ ___ w___
p___ ___ ___ ___ o__ o__ y___
m___ ___, b ___ w ___ i ___ g___ ___ ___
f ___ n ___ ___ ___ ___
e___ ___ ___ ___ ___ ___ ___, t ___ i ___
m ___ i ___ ___ ___ g ___ ___ t__ t___
h ___ ___ ___ ___.

L__ a__ b___ ___ ___ ___ ___ ___ ___,
w___ ___ ___, a___ ___ ___, c___ ___ ___ ___, a___
e___ s___ ___ ___ ___ ___ b__ p___
a___ f ___ ___ y ___, w ___ a___
m___ ___ ___.

A___ b__ k___ ___ t__ o___ ___
a___ ___ ___ ___ ___, t___ ___ ___ ___ ___ ___ ___,
f___ ___ ___ o__ a___ ___ ___,
j___ ___ a__ G__ i__ C___ ___ ___
f___ ___ ___ y__.

KINDNESS

Love in Action

When you think of David, what comes to mind? Do you think of him as king of Israel, the victor over Goliath, the author of many of the Psalms, or just as a shepherd boy chosen by God to replace King Saul? David was all of these.

In addition to all of these stories about David, the Bible tells us about the friendship that existed between David and Jonathan. In many respects, David was no different from any other young person. He wanted to be liked by others and he wanted to have friends.

The strong friendship that bonded David and Jonathan would soon become the reason for one of the greatest acts of kindness recorded in the Bible. The following story explains why kindness is described as "love in action."

Jonathan was the oldest son of Saul, king of Israel. Although he was the natural heir to the throne, Jonathan knew that God had supernaturally chosen his closest friend, David, to be the next king. Out of his obedience to God and friendship with David, Jonathan made a covenant with David and gave him his own robe, tunic, sword, bow and belt. Jonathan acknowledged David's right to the throne by giving him these symbols of royal status.

As David became more popular with the people, especially after slaying Goliath, King Saul sought to kill him. As a result of Saul's jealousy, David had to leave the city and hide in the surrounding countryside. Jonathan and David would meet regularly and Jonathan would tell David of his father's plans. Because of Jonathan's friendship, David was always able to escape from Saul's attempts on his life.

Jonathan was deeply saddened by his father's hatred for David. When they last saw each other, Jonathan said to David, "Show me the kindness of the Lord while I still live. . .you shall not cut off your kindness from my house forever. . ." (1 Samuel 20:14a and15a). In spite of all that his father had done to destroy David, Jonathan asked David to swear that he would never turn his back on his family.

Because of their friendship, David made a covenant with Jonathan that he would always show kindness to his family. David promised that he would not take revenge on Jonathan's family because of what Saul had done to him.

Not long after that covenant was made, the Israelites went into battle against the Philistines at Mount Gilboa. Jonathan, his father Saul and two brothers were killed in the battle. When news of their deaths reached David, he went into great mourning. He grieved over the loss of his best friend.

David assumed the kingship of Israel, but he never forgot Jonathan. He remembered his boyhood friend as an honest person, who did all he could to protect David from his father. Nor did David forget the covenant he made and the kindness he promised to show to Jonathan's family.

Some time later, after David had established the kingdom of Israel, his thoughts drifted back to his loyal and courageous friend. He asked, "Is there still anyone who is left of the house of Saul, that I may show him kindness for Jonathan's sake?" (2 Samuel 9:1).

It was not long before a servant informed David that Jonathan's sole heir was a crippled son named Mephibosheth. As an infant, Mephibosheth had been dropped by his nursemaid as she fled the palace in an effort to save his life. King David immediately called for the young man to be brought to him.

With great fear, Mephibosheth entered the king's presence. Since he was the only surviving son of King Saul's family, he was afraid this new king would want to destroy him. Besides, Mephibosheth was seriously crippled. It was not unusual for rulers to banish from their kingdoms those who had physical deformities.

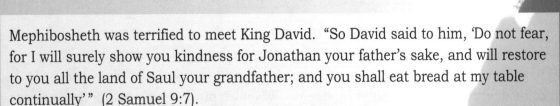

Mephibosheth was terrified to meet King David. "So David said to him, 'Do not fear, for I will surely show you kindness for Jonathan your father's sake, and will restore to you all the land of Saul your grandfather; and you shall eat bread at my table continually'" (2 Samuel 9:7).

Mephibosheth was totally surprised by David's words. To show his humility, Mephibosheth asked, "What is your servant, that you should look upon such a dead dog as I?" (2 Samuel 9:8).

Referring to himself as a "dead dog," Mephibosheth described himself in the worst possible terms. In essence, he was saying that he was an utterly useless person. Not only physically handicapped, Mephibosheth was also the last surviving member of Saul's family. He was of no more use to David than a dead dog and could justifiably be sent to live in the garbage heap outside the city walls.

King David would not accept Mephibosheth's opinion of himself. David saw more than the lame body of a social outcast. In Mephibosheth, he saw one to whom he could repay Jonathan's friendship and kindness. David finally had the opportunity to keep the covenant he had made with Jonathan.

Who are the Mephibosheths in your life?

Stop and think about it. You could be a source of encouragement to a number of people. Some may be handicapped physically, as Mephibosheth was. But it is more likely that there are people around you who feel unloved and unwanted. Every day you pass by students in your school or people in your church or community who feel as if no one cares about them.

There is something they all have in common: They need you. They need your concern, your willingness to be a friend, an encouraging word. They need your kindness.

And what about those you know best, the members of your own family? Are you showing even the simplest of kindnesses to them? Unfortunately, we take for granted those nearest to us, those who have likely done the most for us! Remember, kindness is a fruit of the Spirit-controlled life (Galatians 5:22–23). Because expressing kindness is not something that we "naturally" do, we must look for daily opportunities to show kindness. When we put love into action through our words and deeds, we become a living example of the love of the Lord Jesus Christ.

Finally, what about your own response to God's kindness?

Every day you have a new opportunity to say, "Thank you, Lord, for Your wonderful kindness to me!" If you do this, you will be prepared to think God's way and show His kindness to those who cross your pathway.

Inquiry-Action 30.1

Titus 3:1-8

1. What are the before and after contrasts Paul mentions?

2. What causes a person's life to change from the "before picture" to the "after picture"?

3. Did we have any merit so as to deserve God's kindness? Explain.

4. What are the two aspects of salvation?

5. On what basis should we now live according to the principles of God?

6. What promises do Christians have about the eventual outcome of life?

7. What did Paul want Titus to stress to those who have trusted God?

INQUIRY–ACTION 30.2

"PHONY" KINDNESS

Description	An Example
1) Flattery — dishonestly trying to help others feel good when they may not deserve it.	
2) Compromising a Biblical principle so as not to hurt someone's feelings.	
3) Helping others — (but the real motive is to help ourselves).	

INQUIRY-ACTION 30.2 (CONTINUED)

Description	An Example
4) Giving kindness to others only when kindness is first given to us.	
5) Being kind in order to ease our own feelings of guilt.	

INQUIRY–ACTION 30.3

IDEAS FOR SHOWING KINDNESS

At Home	At School

INQUIRY-ACTION 30.3 (CONTINUED)

To My Friends

_____

_____

_____

_____

_____

To My Neighbors

_____

_____

_____

_____

_____

At Church

_____

_____

_____

_____

To People in General

_____

_____

_____

_____

INQUIRY-ACTION 30.4

RULES OF RELATIONSHIPS

Matthew 7:12

| 1 | 2 | 3 | 4 | 5 | 6 |

Ephesians 6:2

| 1 | 2 | 3 | 4 | 5 | 6 |

Proverbs 17:17

| 1 | 2 | 3 | 4 | 5 | 6 |

Mark 12:31

| 1 | 2 | 3 | 4 | 5 | 6 |

Romans 12:10

| 1 | 2 | 3 | 4 | 5 | 6 |

Luke 6:35

| 1 | 2 | 3 | 4 | 5 | 6 |

INQUIRY-ACTION 30.5

1 PETER 3:8-9   WORD BANK

a	do	love	so
all	evil	may	spirit
and	finally	mind	sum
another	for	might	sympathetic
as	giving	not	tenderhearted
be	harmonious	of	that
because	harmony	on	the
blessing	having	one	thereunto
brethren	humble	or	this
brotherly	in	pitiful	to
brothers	inherit	purpose	up
but	instead	railing	very
called	insult	rendering	were
compassion	kindhearted	repay	with
contrariwise	knowing	returning	ye
contrary	let	reviling	you
courteous	live	should	

RESPECT

Honoring Others in Every Way

Have you ever traveled to a foreign country? If not, you may want to study their customs before you leave home. If you are not well prepared, you could easily embarrass yourself or your host. Here are some "tips" for future travelers:

When in Germany, bring an unwrapped bouquet with an uneven number of flowers (not 13) for your hostess. This demonstrates your appreciation for her hospitality. And remember that only the young and impolite wave at each other from a distance.

When visiting India, whistling under any circumstance is considered impolite; wrap gifts in green, red or yellow (lucky colors), not in black or white (unlucky colors); pointing with a finger is rude (Indians point with their chin); and do not thank your hosts at the end of the meal. Saying "thank you" for a meal is insulting because the thanks are considered a form of payment.

In Japan, the American "OK" sign (thumb and forefinger curled in an "O") means "money." If someone bows to greet you, bow to the same depth in response. The depth of the bow indicates the status of the relationship between you. Finally, when entering a Japanese home, take off your shoes at the door. You will wear a pair of slippers from the door to the living room, where you will remove them. You will put them on again to make your way to the bathroom, where you will exchange them for "toilet slippers." Don't forget to change back again!

What does all of this advice have to do with this week's study? It's simple—respect. Respect is "honoring others in every way." When you are visiting someone else's country, you certainly want to respect their customs and practices.

A recent magazine article began with the following words, "America has become a country in which its citizens have no respect for one another." The author went on to give examples. Drivers cut across lanes of traffic as if the turn-signal had never been invented. Businesses put callers "on hold" for long periods of time. People push in and out of elevators like hockey players facing off over a puck.

George Washington realized, early in his life, the importance of showing respect. As a result, he copied 110 rules in a notebook that he called "Rules of Civility & Decent Behavior in Company and Conversation." Such lists were popular in Colonial times. The following examples are certainly not out of date today:

Rule #4   "In the presence of others, sing not to yourself with a humming noise."
Rule #6   "Sleep not when others speak."
Rule #73   "Think before you speak."
Rule #97   "Put not another bite into your mouth 'til the former be swallowed."
Rule #100   "Cleanse not your teeth with the table cloth."

Washington did more than just copy rules—he lived them. He was especially concerned with rules that emphasized humility, self-control and respect. These were moral lessons that he knew would shape his future.

In 1775 the Continental Congress was so impressed with his character and behavior that it put him in command of the American forces. Twelve years later, Washington was chosen to preside over the convention in Philadelphia, where the Constitution was being debated.

As the first President of the United States, Washington had no established set of rules to follow. However, he did have a model of personal behavior to guide him. The principles he copied into his book became the framework for how he treated others. Respecting his fellow Americans was a stepping stone to recognizing their rights. It's all a matter of Washington's Rule #48, which reminds us that setting a good example influences people more than anything else.

Everyone wants to be respected. Unfortunately, not everyone is. A recent survey asked students, "What characteristics in a person do you respect?" Although there were many answers, the students' responses can be grouped into the following categories:

Consistency: Consistency was ranked as the most important characteristic of people who are respected. These people do not tell one story to one person and a different story to someone else. They also can be counted on to do what they say they will do. Consistent people stand by you—no matter what anyone else says!

Authenticity: People who are respected are not fakes. They don't try to impress you with how strong, smart or talented they are. They don't try to "use" you to make themselves look better. Authentic people are not consumed with themselves. They are confident that God is at work in their lives.

Unselfishness: Those whom we respect the most watch out for themselves the least! They notice the needs of others and reach out to help, honestly concerned about the welfare of others. Their least used words are "I," "me," "my" and "mine." They are unselfish.

Tirelessness: Respect always goes to those who will not quit. No matter how difficult the task becomes, these people will never give up. Their enthusiasm and desire to succeed is infectious. As a result, you will never hear these people say the words, "It's too hard."

Are you respected by others? Or, put a different way, do you have a reputation you can be proud of?

There are some individuals who could probably do the cause of Christ a lot of good by not telling people that they are Christians. There are others who act so "holy" that no one wants to be around them. If you have ever watched a wildlife show on TV, you may have seen sucker fishes (called remoras) that attach themselves to sharks and whales. Your reputation is like a remora. It's stuck to you and everything related to you. Getting rid of a bad reputation, like a remora, is very hard to do.

Being a person others respect requires a lifelong commitment to excellence. A first step is showing respect to others.

In order for your quest for character to be successful, you must learn to honor God and others. In other words, respect should characterize your relationships with those around you. As you learn to respect others, others will grow in their respect for you.

Respect for others begins with respect for God and His Word. Note what the Psalmist said about the relationship between God's Word and respect:

> "How can a young man cleanse his way? By taking heed according to Your word." (Psalm 119:9)

> "Your word I have hidden in my heart, that I might not sin against You." (Psalm 119:11)

> "I will meditate on Your precepts, and contemplate Your ways." (Psalm 119:15)

As you demonstrate respect for God and His Word, you will also have respect for others. As a result, others will soon respect you. It all begins with your relationship to Him.

INQUIRY-ACTION 31.1

"HOW WOULD YOU LIKE FOR ME TO SHOW RESPECT?"

Record the answers from people listed below.

Mom: _____

_____

_____

_____

Dad: _____

_____

_____

_____

Elderly Person: _____

_____

_____

_____

INQUIRY–ACTION 31.1 (CONTINUED)

Teacher, Coach or Pastor: _____

_____

_____

_____

Employer: _____

_____

_____

_____

Government Official: _____

_____

_____

_____

INQUIRY-ACTION 31.2

I.   As we honor others, we show them respect (Romans 12:10–13:7).

_____

_____

_____

_____

II.   Respect is based on the fact that God created us in His image and likeness (Genesis 1:26 ff).

_____

_____

_____

_____

III.   Civilized societies are based on mutual respect (1 Peter 2:13–17).

_____

_____

_____

_____

INQUIRY–ACTION 31.2 (CONTINUED)

IV. We show respect to others by:

- listening and being polite

- obeying laws and rules

- being considerate of others' feelings, ideas and actions

- _____

- _____

- _____

- _____

- _____

- _____

- _____

- _____

- _____

INQUIRY-ACTION 31.3

SUGGESTIONS FOR DEVELOPING AND KEEPING SELF-RESPECT

1. Develop a right relationship with God.

_____

_____

_____

_____

2. Keep your life free of sin.

_____

_____

_____

_____

3. Keep right relationships with other people.

_____

_____

_____

_____

INQUIRY–ACTION 31.3 (CONTINUED)

HOW I CAN EARN THE RESPECT OF OTHERS

1. Consistency

_____

_____

_____

2. Authenticity

_____

_____

_____

3. Unselfishness

_____

_____

_____

4. Tirelessness

_____

_____

_____

According to Luke 6:35, the bottom line is:

_____

_____

_____

INQUIRY-ACTION 31.4

1 PETER 2:15–17: WORD SEARCH

Use your Bible, or your memory, to locate all the words in the giant word-find.
Copy the verses at the bottom.

```
C O V E R U P E H T H I S E C N E L I S D O G A
T N A R O N G I Z H A S H O W C L O A K E C I V
R O F U T O N E M A Y T A L K I N G O D L U H S
A G O D S E R V I T T I L I W A N T C E P S E R
E O R L O V E D O I N G O D S M P E O P L E W E
F O O L I S H B U T O N E M S E R H O N O R E V
R D O G B Q T H E H T O F O R U S T U P V A N E
E O D L D Y O U V A H R E P O R P A S V E L O I
E T L O W E F R E T T A S Y T R E B I L A L Y L
R I G O E T O O R B O N D S E R V A N T S I R E
W O H S S T X N E M F C O D A S D O G L O V E B
I S H O U L D O N E A E V I L T O F I T H E V Y
L T U B R O T H E R H O O D M O D E E R F Y E T
```

_____

_____

_____

_____

_____

_____

_____

LEADERSHIP

Character Which Inspires Confidence

If you go to your local bookstore, you will find many books on the topic of leadership. Contained within each of those books would be a definition of leadership. Although all of the definitions would probably differ in some way, the core principle of each definition would be the same: Leadership is influence! To the degree that you are able to influence others, you are able to lead them.

That's exactly what Lord Montgomery meant when he wrote:

> "Leadership is the capacity and will to rally men and women to
> a common purpose, and the character which inspires confidence."

A group of young leaders was asked to list qualities or characteristics found in leaders. Their list included the following:

knowledge	optimism	decisiveness
independence	integrity	aggressiveness
enthusiasm	competitiveness	persistence
flexibility	sense of humor	inquisitiveness
discipline	insight	practicality

You will surely agree that these qualities are found in "natural" leaders. In your history classes you have already studied the lives of many men and women who demonstrated these characteristics in important leadership positions. But should these qualities be the focus of our study of leadership? In other words, are these qualities absolutely necessary in a "spiritual" leader too?

If you stop for a moment and think about it, there are a number of Biblical leaders who would have done poorly on a test of "natural" leadership skills.

First, there was Moses. When you think of Moses, you probably think of the account of the plagues, the parting of the Red Sea or the receiving of the Ten Commandments. These were all spectacular events. Based on these events, it would be easy to conclude that Moses was naturally a great and influential leader.

But what about the Moses described in Exodus 3:10–4:14? He is described in this passage as withdrawn, insecure, fearful and doubting. He had a speech impairment that made it difficult to communicate. Certainly he was not by natural talents the type of leader described earlier in this chapter.

There was also the prophet Amos. He was mightily used of God to warn Israel and the surrounding nations of God's coming judgment of their sins. However, he is described in 7:10–17 as lacking culture, being negative, not liked, poorly prepared and clumsy. The description of Amos certainly does not fit the modern definition of a leader.

Finally, consider Peter. He was certainly a great speaker, an effective writer and someone who desired to follow the Lord. But as you follow his life through the pages of the New Testament, you realize that he was impulsive, boastful and frequently said things when he should have kept his mouth shut.

This is not to say that Moses, Amos and Peter did not have "natural" leadership capabilities. It's just that most people would not have thought of them as the typical "model" leader. That is because God looks for other qualities of leadership—qualities that are far more important than the list provided at the beginning of this chapter.

More than anything else, God looks for those who love Him and make themselves available to do His will. Once we surrender ourselves to Him, He gives us the basic ingredients of faith, vision and determination needed to accomplish great things for Him.

God is also looking for those who are willing to serve others. This is the second characteristic of leadership that is seldom mentioned but is highly valued by God. The Bible clearly teaches that he who desires to lead must first be willing to serve.

This principle is clearly taught in John 13. As Jesus was preparing His disciples for their future ministry, He took a towel and began to wash their feet (verse 5).

This custom was clearly understood by the disciples. Washing the feet of another was only done by the lowest of servants. When Jesus started to wash their feet, Peter immediately resisted, not wanting the Lord to humble Himself in this way. Peter knew that he was not worthy to have his feet washed by the Lord.

Jesus used the example of washing feet to teach His disciples a very important lesson. If we are unwilling to humble ourselves and serve others, we are not fit to lead others. Someone who willingly washed the feet of another demonstrated humility and servanthood. The Bible makes it very clear that God is looking for leaders who are willingly available to Him and are humble servants.

This is certainly not the picture of leadership portrayed in the world today. Godly leadership is not like the self-centered, power-hungry executives characterized on television and in the movies. Godly leadership is characterized by influence that directs others to honor God through their words and actions. In order to influence others in this way, our lives must be characterized by humble obedience.

If your desire is to lead others, there is a very important question you must ask yourself. "Will my leadership be characterized by godly or worldly standards?" Don't kid yourself! God's pattern for leading others is very different from the world's.

If it is your desire to lead, be a leader who stands apart from all the rest. That's the challenge that the Lord puts before you today. To be a godly leader, you must determine to take the following steps:

1) Express to the Lord that you are making yourself available to Him. Indicate your willingness to trust and obey Him in all things.

2) Learn what it means to be a servant. Look for opportunities at school and at home to serve others.

Remember, leadership is a combination of abilities and character. But the best abilities are **availability** and **dependability**.

INQUIRY-ACTION 32.1

LEADERSHIP NOTES

1. The central word expressing true leadership is _____ others to take certain actions.

2. Five qualities generally thought to be important for leaders are . . .

_____

_____

_____

_____

_____

3. God does not always choose leaders with _____ talents and abilities.

4. Moses was a great leader, but his early life was characterized by . . .

_____

_____

_____

5. Amos was a strong prophet, but his background included . . .

_____

_____

_____

INQUIRY–ACTION 32.1 (CONTINUED)

6. Peter became one of the two important leaders of the early church. However, he had some very "unleadership-like" qualities, including . . .

_____

_____

_____

7. Jesus showed that a leader must be a servant by . . .

_____

_____

_____

8. Some advice for those who want to become leaders is . . .

_____

_____

_____

INQUIRY-ACTION 32.2

BIBLICAL LEADERS

Leader: _____

References: _____

What the leader is most known for: _____

_____

_____

_____

Qualities or actions thought to be uncharacteristic of leaders: _____

_____

_____

_____

_____

Lessons to be learned: _____

_____

_____

_____

_____

INQUIRY–ACTION 32.3

WHAT MAKES A GOOD LEADER

1. Have a Respected Reputation

2. Be Responsible to Family

3. Be Self-Controlled

4. Be a Good Thinker

5. Be Concerned for Others

6. Be Able to Teach Others

7. Not Be Negative or Violent

8. Not Be Self-Serving

INQUIRY–ACTION 32.4

THINGS I NEED TO DO

---

1. Have a Respected Reputation

---

2. Be Responsible to Family

---

3. Be Self-Controlled

---

4. Be a Good Thinker

---

5. Be Concerned for Others

---

6. Be Able to Teach Others

---

7. Not Be Negative or Violent

---

8. Not Be Self-Serving

INQUIRY-ACTION 32.5

MATTHEW 20:25-28

INQUIRY-ACTION 32.5 (CONTINUED)

INQUIRY–ACTION 32.5 (CONTINUED)

      2

  2 **+** **2**

 A **4** .

COMMITMENT

Determined to Do What Is Right

When was the last time you opened your dictionary just to see what was there? If you're like most people, probably never! That's because the dictionary is a resource that is designed to help you communicate. If you use a dictionary properly, you will be able to select appropriate words to express your feelings and thoughts.

The typical dictionary contains thousands of words that you will probably never read or hear in your entire lifetime. A perfect example is the word "gimp." A very famous preacher used the word "gimp" to create a new word, "gimper."

According to the originator, a gimper is not a rare type of bird, an endangered species of animal or a unique kind of fish. However, there are occasional sightings of gimpers on school campuses, in office buildings, in churches, at home and on athletic teams. In fact, though their appearances are rare, gimpers form the back-bone of whatever they're a part of. One of the reasons they are so hard to find is that they are never found in groups. Gimpers are loners. Some are very famous; others are unknown.

So, what is a gimper? Although the word "gimper" is not in the dictionary, "gimp" is. It means "spirit," "vigor," "ambition." The word "gimper" was first used by the famous radio preacher, Dr. M. R. DeHaan, to refer to someone who "excels, is different, is committed to the core." Gimpers set their sights high. No matter what the obstacles, they are committed to reaching their goals.

Can you think of some famous gimpers? Here are a few that are certainly familiar.

- A gimper president was Abraham Lincoln.
- Jim Elliot was a gimper missionary.
- As a gimper baseball player, Jackie Robinson stands out.
- Thomas Edison was clearly a gimper inventor.
- Heather Whitestone was a gimper Miss America.

No matter what the obstacles, these individuals would not give up. They were committed to doing what was right, committed to accomplishing their goals.

Did the Lord Jesus ever talk about gimpers? He certainly did. A number of the obvious examples are found in the Sermon on the Mount (Matthew 5). Note how the Lord encourages us to be gimpers.

- If someone smites them on the cheek, gimpers turn the other cheek (verse 39).
- If someone sues them and takes them to court, gimpers let that person have the rest of their garments (verse 40).
- If someone wants him or her to go a mile, the gimper goes two miles (verse 41).
- Although some love their friends and hate their enemies, gimpers love their enemies and pray for their persecutors.

Gimpers are so committed that they excel in everything they do. While the average Christian rejoices sometimes, gimper Christians "rejoice always." While it is true that most Christians pray, gimpers "pray without ceasing." Although it is common to give thanks, gimpers give thanks "in everything." Certainly Christians try to avoid evil. However, gimper believers "abstain from every appearance of evil." While most people try to overcome difficulties, gimpers are "more than conquerors" through Jesus Christ.

The lesson is clear. Gimpers are absolutely committed. They are wholehearted about everything they do. They excel. They never give up. They are absolutely determined to finish a task—and to do it right!

If you have ever seen a football game, you have watched the players go into a huddle. During those few seconds, they determine the strategy for the next play. Then someone yells, "BREAK!" The players come out of the huddle, advance toward the opposing team and prepare to execute the chosen play.

But suppose the next time that you are watching a football game, you notice something unusual. Although the teams look the same as before, one of the teams does not seem to be aggressive.

This less aggressive team finally gets possession of the football. Behind by three touchdowns, the team goes into its huddle. As the moments tick by, the fans anxiously wait for play to begin. But the team doesn't move. A couple of minutes go by, and the referee penalizes the team for taking too much time. Even that doesn't seem to have any effect. No one comes out of the huddle. Matter of fact, the team finally announces that it is going to stay in the huddle.

"Absurd!," you say. "The huddle is a time to plan, encourage each other and prepare to face the opposing team. It is of no use to go into the huddle if you are unwilling to get into the game." It's the same with life. Don't hold back. Don't just sit on the bench. Get into the game!

Josiah was certainly not afraid to "get into the game." Judah had been ruled by wicked kings for over 60 years when, at the age of eight, Josiah came to the throne. As he neared manhood, Josiah "began to seek the God of his father David" (2 Chronicles 34:3).

At the age of 20, Josiah removed the idols from the altars and began repairs on the Jerusalem Temple. It was during the repairs that he found a copy of the Law. He learned upon reading the Law that Judah had failed to obey the Lord. As the country's leader, he "tore his robes" in an act of humility and repentance.

Josiah then committed himself to leading the nation in revival. He completely cleansed his land of the idols, false worship centers and pagan religious leaders. The nation once again celebrated Passover and the other feasts and festivals commanded by God. As a result of Josiah's commitment, the nation of Judah returned to the Lord.

Josiah was a "gimper" king. He was determined to do what was right. No matter what the obstacles, nothing was going to stop him from doing the will of God.

Think about the football illustration used earlier in this chapter. Would you agree that there are some Christians who always seem to be in the huddle and never in the game?

Some Christians spend all of their time planning, encouraging each other and preparing to play. But when it comes right down to action, they don't make the commitment to get into the game.

Are you in the huddle, or in the game? "Commit your way to the Lord, trust also in Him; and He shall bring it to pass" (Psalm 37:5).

Inquiry-Action 33.1

Personal Evaluation

Directions: Be honest with yourself. Only you will look at your evaluation.

Circle the level that best shows how you manage this area of commitment.

	Almost Never					Always
1. I keep my promises.	0%	20%	40%	60%	80%	100%
2. Once I decide the right thing to do, nothing can make me do wrong.	0%	20%	40%	60%	80%	100%
3. I always do/go exactly as I tell my parents.	0%	20%	40%	60%	80%	100%
4. I am known as a person who keeps his/her word.	0%	20%	40%	60%	80%	100%
5. People know they can depend on me.	0%	20%	40%	60%	80%	100%
6. If I start something, you can be sure I'll finish it.	0%	20%	40%	60%	80%	100%
7. I do my regular chores without being reminded.	0%	20%	40%	60%	80%	100%
8. I complete my assignments and homework without being reminded.	0%	20%	40%	60%	80%	100%
9. I am always on time.	0%	20%	40%	60%	80%	100%
10. I can be trusted to keep a secret.	0%	20%	40%	60%	80%	100%

INQUIRY–ACTION 33.1 (CONTINUED)

	Almost Never					Always
11. I am known as a person who tells the truth.	0%	20%	40%	60%	80%	100%
12. I have a lot of self-determination.	0%	20%	40%	60%	80%	100%
13. I am known as a person who never gives up—who never quits.	0%	20%	40%	60%	80%	100%
14. It's easy for me to resist negative peer pressure.	0%	20%	40%	60%	80%	100%
15. I am known as a person who consistently tries to do right.	0%	20%	40%	60%	80%	100%
16. I consistently show my parents that I am responsible and trustworthy.	0%	20%	40%	60%	80%	100%
17. I am careful about my schedule and hardly ever waste time.	0%	20%	40%	60%	80%	100%
18. I am faithful to read my Bible and pray daily.	0%	20%	40%	60%	80%	100%
19. I regularly attend church activities.	0%	20%	40%	60%	80%	100%
20. I am determined to do what God wants.	0%	20%	40%	60%	80%	100%

INQUIRY-ACTION 33.2

COMMITMENT INVOLVES:

INQUIRY-ACTION 33.2 (CONTINUED)

The area least needing improvement: (Underline one.)

The area most needing improvement: (Underline one.)

  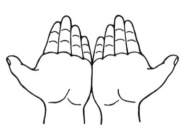

What I need to do: _____

_____

_____

_____

_____

INQUIRY-ACTION 33.3
THE APOSTLE PAUL

Committed to Opposing God's Work

_____

_____

_____

_____

_____

_____

_____

Committed to Knowing Christ

_____

_____

_____

_____

_____

INQUIRY-ACTION 33.3 (CONTINUED)

Committed to Living by Faith

_____

_____

_____

_____

_____

Committed to Preaching Christ

_____

_____

_____

_____

_____

Committed to Service until Death

_____

_____

_____

_____

_____

Inquiry–Action 33.4

PSALM 37:4–5

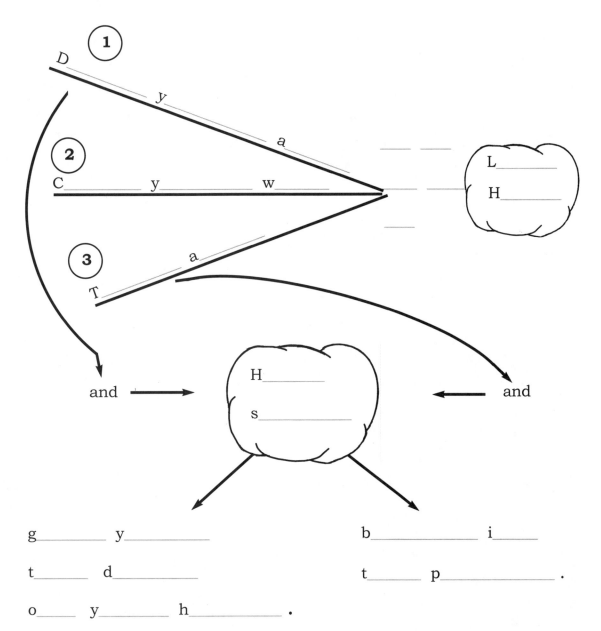

(1) D_____ y_____ a_____

(2) C_____ y_____ w_____

L_____
H_____

(3) T_____ a_____

and →

H_____
s_____

← and

g_____ y_____
t_____ d_____
o_____ y_____ h_____ .

b_____ i_____
t_____ p_____ .

SERVICE

Investing Your Life in Others

There are only two bodies of water in Israel, the Dead Sea and the Sea of Galilee. Both bodies of water play a significant role in the history of God's people and the nation.

The Sea of Galilee is a large, fresh water lake in the northern part of the country. This body of water is called by a variety of names in the Bible: Sea of Kinnereth (Joshua 12:3), Lake of Gennesaret (Luke 5:1) and the Sea of Tiberias (John 6:1). Much of the Lord's ministry took place on the shores and in the cities surrounding the Sea of Galilee.

To the south is the Dead Sea, which has the lowest altitude of any body of water in the world. It is an oblong lake, three-fourths as long as the Jordan Valley north of it. Fifty miles in length, the widest part of the Dead Sea is no more than 18 miles.

Archaeologists believe that the region surrounding the Dead Sea was once a fertile, desirable place to live. That changed during the time of Lot. Sodom and Gomorrah were probably located at the southern end of the Dead Sea. When the Lord reduced them to rubble because of their wickedness (Genesis 19), an earthquake probably dropped the land on which the cities stood, and the waters of the Dead Sea were formed.

Since that time, the Dead Sea and the surrounding region have been a desolate wasteland. Even the fish struggle against being carried into the sea, because its high mineral content brings immediate death. The waters are so thick and oily that nothing sinks—even people easily float on top of the water.

Although the Sea of Galilee and the Dead Sea are approximately 60 miles apart and are connected by the Jordan River, they have little else in common. As a fresh water lake, the Sea of Galilee takes in water from other rivers as well as allowing water to flow from it to other destinations. That is what is meant when it is described as a "fresh water" lake. It literally teems with life. Fish abound and are the major source of local economy.

On the other hand, the Dead Sea is a lifeless body of water. The reason is simple. The Dead Sea takes in water but never gives it out. The water remains and stagnates. As a result, no fish or plant life are able to survive in its waters.

The comparison of the Sea of Galilee and the Dead Sea provides an excellent illustration of this week's topic: service. Think of a person as one of the two seas. He receives from others such things as friendship, instruction, assistance in times of need and special gifts. When he is willing to give out these same things in return, he is like the Sea of Galilee, living and fresh. His life is making a positive contribution to all that it touches.

However, if he is always taking in from others and never giving anything back, he is like the lifeless Dead Sea. Never using what he has received to serve others, he stagnates. "Sit, soak and sour!" could be his life's motto. Although he knows and has so much, his life has no impact on the lives of others.

Taking in so you can invest your life in others is at the heart of service. Why is it that we are so unwilling to serve others? The reason is self-centeredness.

The "ME" generation describes today's young people. This generation has been characterized as only concerned about what they have and what others will do for them, with little or no concern for the needs or welfare of others. In a word, this generation has been described as selfish.

Although people have always been selfish (Genesis 13:10–11; Luke 10:30–32), self-centeredness seems to be clearly on the increase in our society. A quick look at the daily newspaper or any of the many weekly magazines should convince you of man's self-centeredness. The words of 2 Timothy 3:1–2 seem to be coming true right before our very eyes, "But know this, that in the last days perilous times will come: For men will be lovers of themselves . . . ."

Investing your life in others can never happen if your life is characterized by self-centeredness. This principle was clearly demonstrated by the life of Gladys Aylward.

③

While the Germans were bombing London during World War I, young Gladys Aylward would gather the children off the street and bring them into her home. There she would sing hymns as loud as she could so that the noise of the bombs could not be heard by the children. Even at a young age, Gladys Aylward was already focused on serving others, not centered upon herself.

When the opportunity came for her to enroll in the China Inland Mission School in London, she did so immediately. In her mind, China provided unlimited opportunities for service. But after a few months, she was asked to leave the school. Her academic work, especially in the area of theology, was not going well. Her teachers believed that she would never be able to learn the Chinese language.

Although Miss Aylward left the school, she never gave up her goal to go to China. She soon learned of an elderly missionary, named Jennie Lawson, who wanted a younger woman to take over her work in northern China. She applied for the position and was told if she could raise the money to get to China, the position was hers. Miss Aylward was soon on her way to China.

The next few years were difficult as the two women labored throughout the countryside. They opened an Inn in Yangcheng in order to support their work and to spread the word of the Gospel through the mule drivers who stopped there. It was not long after they established the Inn that Miss Lawson died. Gladys Aylward carried on the work of the Inn of Eight Happinesses. (You might remember the motion picture *Inn of the Sixth Happiness* that portrayed this work.)

Soon Miss Aylward again turned her attention to the children. Establishing orphanages throughout the country, she was greatly admired by the Chinese. But it was her service during World War II that brought her worldwide fame. Leading a band of almost 100 children, Gladys Aylward walked hundreds of miles through the mountains to escape the enemy soldiers and secure safety for the children.

Although she completed the journey and delivered the children to safety, her health was seriously damaged by the hardships of the trip. She had contracted pneumonia, suffered from malnutrition, typhus and relapsing fever. However, God delivered her from all of these diseases. For the next ten years she traveled throughout England to raise money for the many orphanages she had established. She then returned to China to serve the people—especially the children! In 1970 she went home to be with the Lord. For her entire life, Gladys Aylward had invested her life in the lives of others.

Society says, "You are the single most important person in your life. You must consider your own happiness above anyone else's. You deserve whatever you want." The focus is always on you; the trend is total self-centeredness. On the contrary, Christians know that selfishness is not the pathway to obedience and happiness. Like the Dead Sea, if you always take in and never give out, you will become lifeless and useless. God has a better way.

④

The message of the Bible is clear: Consider the interests and needs of others. Be a servant in all that you do. Perhaps the most famous Bible passage about being selfless is Philippians 2:3–7: "Let nothing be done through selfish ambition or conceit, but in lowliness of mind let each esteem others better than himself. Let each of you look out not only for his own interests, but also for the interests of others. Let this mind be in you which was also in Christ Jesus, who . . . made Himself of no reputation, taking the form of a bondservant . . . ."

Service, investing your life in others, is a central theme throughout the Bible. Is it a character trait that is evident in your life? If not, begin today to look outward—not inward!

INQUIRY-ACTION 34.1

SERVANT-LEADERSHIP

An unpleasant task I am committing to perform . . .

* at home: _____

_____

Reaction: _____

* at school: _____

_____

Reaction: _____

* at church: _____

_____

Reaction: _____

INQUIRY-ACTION 34.1 (CONTINUED)

THREE EXAMPLES OF SERVANT-LEADERSHIP

Who? What happened?

1. _____

_____

_____

_____

_____

2. _____

_____

_____

_____

_____

3. _____

_____

_____

_____

_____

INQUIRY-ACTION 34.2

JOB DESCRIPTION FOR MY PERSONAL SERVANT

Have you ever written a job description? Now's your chance! Suppose that you had a personal servant. In the space below, list the tasks that you would require your servant to do for you:

1. _____

_____

_____

2. _____

_____

_____

3. _____

_____

_____

4. _____

_____

_____

5. _____

_____

_____

INQUIRY-ACTION 34.2 (CONTINUED)

Based on what I would like someone to do for me, some things I should be willing to do for someone else are:

1. _____

_____

_____

2. _____

_____

_____

3. _____

_____

_____

4. _____

_____

_____

5. _____

_____

_____

Inquiry-Action 34.3

Being a Servant

I. Some Notable Servants in the Bible:

_____   _____

_____   _____

II. Types of Servants:

A. Slave – _____

_____

B. Hireling (hired servant) – _____

_____

C. Servant – _____

_____

D. Bondservant – _____

_____

INQUIRY-ACTION 34.3 (CONTINUED)

III. Marks of a Servant

    A. _____

    _____

    _____

    B. _____

    _____

    _____

    C. _____

    _____

    _____

IV. Lesson for Me: _____

_____

_____

_____

INQUIRY-ACTION 34.4

LEARNING TO BE A SERVANT

Assignment: _____

Scripture: _____

1. What are the main points of this story or passage? _____

_____

_____

2. What were the marks of a servant and how were they shown? _____

_____

_____

3. What personal lessons should be learned from this passage? _____

_____

_____

4. Plan for presentation: _____

_____

_____

INQUIRY-ACTION 34.5

MY LIFE INVESTED IN OTHERS

In the space provided, list ten specific ways that you can invest your life in the lives of others:

1. _____

2. _____

3. _____

4. _____

5. _____

6. _____

7. _____

8. _____

9. _____

10. _____

INQUIRY-ACTION 34.5 (CONTINUED)

MY PERSONAL INVESTMENT PORTFOLIO

From your list of the ten ways that you can invest your life in the lives of others, select two of your choices for your personal investment portfolio.

INVESTMENT CHOICE: _____

How will this choice benefit others? _____

_____

_____

How can God use this choice to fulfill His plan in my life? _____

_____

_____

What are the "dividends" that I will expect to receive? _____

_____

_____

What will happen if I don't make this investment? _____

_____

_____

INQUIRY–ACTION 34.5 (CONTINUED)

INVESTMENT CHOICE: _____

How will this choice benefit others? _____

_____

_____

How can God use this choice to fulfill His plan in my life? _____

_____

_____

What are the "dividends" that I will expect to receive? _____

_____

_____

What will happen if I don't make this investment? _____

_____

_____

Inquiry-Action 34.6

Titus 2:9a and 10b

Write the words of the verses down the left side. On the right explain, define or write synonyms for each word.

1. _____ _____

2. _____ _____

3. _____ _____

4. _____ _____

5. _____ _____

6. _____ _____

7. _____ _____

8. _____ _____

9. _____ _____

10. _____ _____

11. _____ _____

12. _____ _____

13. _____ _____

14. _____ _____

Inquiry-Action 34.6 (CONTINUED)

15. _____   _____

16. . . .   *(an ellipsis showing words were skipped)*

17. _____   _____

18. _____   _____

19. _____   _____

20. _____   _____

21. _____   _____

22. _____   _____

23. _____   _____

24. _____   _____

25. _____   _____

26. _____   _____

27. _____   _____

28. _____   _____

29. _____   _____

REVERENCE

Honoring God through Our Worship

One day Moses was out in the desert looking after his father-in-law's sheep when he noticed a strange sight. He saw a bush burning. Now there is nothing strange about a bush on fire. What was strange was that the bush was not burning up. It was not being consumed. It was not turning to ashes. That was very unusual!

So, he walked toward the bush to take a closer look. All of a sudden, God spoke to him from the middle of the bush. "Don't come any closer, Moses. Take off your sandals. You are standing on holy ground."

The ground where Moses was standing didn't look any different from the ground all around it—rugged, very sandy and full of weeds. There were the normal desert animals and plenty of bugs! It certainly looked like ordinary desert dirt. What was God talking about? Surely He was not suggesting that this was some kind of extra-special dirt.

No, God meant that it was ordinary ground that was different because He had set it apart for His special purposes. That's what God meant when He said it was "holy" ground. Holy means "set apart." It was a place God had chosen to meet Moses. It was also a place where Moses could honor and worship God.

The "burning bush" experience illustrates what it means to show reverence. Reverence is acknowledging God for Who He is through both honor and worship. Let's begin by reviewing the formal acts of reverence described in the Bible. Then let's consider the informal, or personal, responses of reverence that we can show. Finally we will look at how one man's reverence has affected the lives of thousands.

The Old Testament gives many examples of how the people of Israel, as a whole, were to demonstrate their reverence for God. The system of sacrifices and offerings, festivals and feasts were all a part of the formal acts of honoring God. There were also prescribed rituals, such as the Day of Atonement, when the entire nation of Israel expressed its needs and appreciation to God.

In the New Testament, the system of sacrifices, offerings, festivals, feasts and rituals are absent from the worship of the church. In the Old Testament, the emphasis of worship was on the "service" performed by the priests and Levites. But after the Lord's earthly ministry, death and resurrection, the New Testament church realized that the worship system of the Old Testament had been fulfilled in Jesus Christ. Reverence was now to be shown by presenting our bodies as living sacrifices, as Paul said, "which is your reasonable service" (Romans 12:1).

Although Old Testament expressions of reverence were primarily through the formal acts of sacrifices, offerings, etc., there were also examples of personal acts of worship. Abraham's servant praised God for answering his prayers (Genesis 24:26, 27). Jacob erected an altar to celebrate his vision of God (Genesis 28:10–22). Hannah's psalm of praise is one of the most beautiful expressions of personal worship found in the Bible (I Samuel 2:1–10). Then, of course, there are the Psalms. If you want to learn how to express your love for God, the Psalms provide the perfect model.

More examples of personal acts of worship are described in the New Testament. Believers gathered together to praise God, sing to Him and offer prayers. Paul frequently begins his letters with expressions of praise and honor for God (e.g., Ephesians 1:3–10). Reverence was expressed in the early church through worship that honored God.

As you can see, the worship and praise of God is a major theme in the Bible. Each time that you go to church, you have the opportunity to freely and openly express your love and thanks to God. When you honor Him, you are showing reverence.

There are many people in the world who do not have the opportunity to freely and openly worship God. One such place is Guangzhou, China.

Throughout Communist China, a revival is taking place called the "house church" movement. Under Communism, religion is only allowed when conducted according to the guidelines of the government. In this way, what churches do and say can be strictly regulated.

It is estimated that 90% of the believers in China worship in unregistered house churches. As a result, many are persecuted by the government. No one knows the exact number of these house churches, but it is probably in the thousands.

China's best known house church is in Guangzhou. It is led by Pastor Samuel Lamb. Pastor Lamb, who is 72, has served more than 21 years in prison for his faith. Fifteen of his prison years were imposed because he tried to copy a New Testament. During this 15-year imprisonment, his wife died; and his mother died within a few months after he left prison. When asked how he could bear such persecution, he said, "You must have a mind to suffer. If you have a mind to suffer, you can stand it. But if you don't have a mind to suffer, you can be broken."

God has been honored and glorified through Pastor Lamb's personal testimony. His desire to be obedient and his reverence for God have had a profound impact on the people in Guangzhou.

Over the years, the government has closed his house church and confiscated his property many times. Yet every time a house church is closed down, it reappears in another location. It has now come to the point that China's government leaves him alone. Why? "Each time they arrested me and sent me off to prison, the church grew," Pastor Lamb explained. "Persecution was good for us. The more they persecuted, the more the church grew." Pastor Lamb's life is a practical illustration of reverence for God.

Reverence, honoring God through our worship, can take place in both formal and informal ways. There are many examples of formal acts of worship in the Bible, especially in the Old Testament. Although the sacrifices, festivals, etc., are not practiced today, they help us understand God and His Word.

Praise, singing and prayers are just a few of the personal, informal ways that we can honor God through our worship. But more importantly, we must remember that how we live our lives best shows our reverence for God. Pastor Samuel Lamb is certainly an excellent example. Whether in the house church or in the prison, God has been honored by Pastor's Lamb's life. His reverence and devotion to God have caused the faith of others to be strengthened.

It was not the burning bush that surprised Moses the most that day on the mountain. Moses was most surprised when God told him that the sandy, bug-infested dirt on which he was standing was "holy ground." Of course the dirt was not holy ground; it was the fact that Moses was in the presence of God.

When we attend church, go to chapel, bow in prayer or study God's Word, we have also entered into His presence. Just like Moses, we are standing on "holy ground." As we honor God through our worship, we show reverence for Him through our attitudes, words and actions.

INQUIRY-ACTION 35.1

WE SHOULD SHOW REVERENCE TO GOD BECAUSE OF . . .

Who He Is

1. _____

_____

2. _____

_____

3. _____

_____

4. _____

_____

5. _____

_____

What He Has Done

1. _____

_____

2. _____

_____

3. _____

_____

4. _____

_____

5. _____

_____

INQUIRY-ACTION 35.2

READING NOTES FOR CHAPTER 35

1. What caused Moses to reverence God?

_____

_____

_____

2. How did believers in the Old Testament worship God?

_____

_____

_____

_____

3. How did believers in the New Testament worship God?

_____

_____

_____

_____

4. How do the "house church" and Pastor Lamb show reverence for God?

_____

_____

_____

INQUIRY-ACTION 35.2 (CONTINUED)

5. Thumb through the Psalms and list three references that show reverence to God.

_____

_____

_____

6. Name a part of your church worship and describe how it shows reverence to God.

_____

_____

_____

7. Write a personal application from this chapter.

_____

_____

_____

INQUIRY-ACTION 35.3

Dear Pastor _____,

This week in Bible class, we have been studying the need to show reverence to God. Some

things I have learned are:

_____

_____

_____

_____

_____

_____

_____

_____

_____

_____

_____

_____

_____

_____

_____

INQUIRY-ACTION 35.3 (CONTINUED)

On the basis of our study of reverence, I plan to make some practical applications.   These
include: _____

_____

_____

_____

_____

_____

Thanks for your ministry, especially the way you _____

_____

_____

_____

Please pray for me as I put into practice the things I know are right.

Sincerely,

INQUIRY-ACTION 35.4

1. **Regarding** _____

I plan to show reverence by _____

_____

_____

2. **Regarding** _____

I plan to show reverence by _____

_____

_____

3. **Regarding** _____

I plan to show reverence by _____

_____

_____

4. **Regarding** _____

I plan to show reverence by _____

_____

_____

INQUIRY-ACTION 35.5

HEBREWS 12:28

_____

_____

_____

_____

_____

_____

_____

_____

_____

_____

_____

_____

_____

_____

_____

_____

Syllable Bank	
king	en
re	fear
we	be
cept	ful
un	ate
there	us
can	ship
ceir	less
er	shak
with	ly
since	wor
that	ver
fore	let
ing	tion
dom	God
re	and
not	ed
are	thank
bly	ac
ence	es
a	so
con	pro
de	y

REVIEW

Highlights of *Character Quest Volume 2*

YOUR QUEST HAS JUST BEGUN!

Quest is certainly an interesting word. A person on a quest is on a journey with a specific objective in mind. It is an exciting adventure marked by a determination to reach a goal. Those involved experience a sense of destiny as they achieve their purpose regardless of the cost or hardship. As you reflect on this past school year, you realize that you have been on a very specific journey. You have been on a *Character Quest!*

Stop for a moment and think about the many famous journeys that have taken place over the centuries. Both the Bible and your history book record many important historical journeys. Probably the first one that comes to mind is the journey of Abraham.

Abraham was born nearly 4,100 years ago in the Mesopotamian city of Ur. According to Joshua 24:2, he rejected the worship of the "other gods" to give himself to Jehovah. It was Jehovah God who told him to leave Ur and travel to an unknown land. Abraham's journey took him along well-established trade routes, first to Haran—where his father died—and then on to Canaan.

Abraham's journey was not just a physical caravan from Ur to Canaan, however. It was a spiritual journey as well. God had told Abraham that he would not only inherit a new country, but he would also be the father of a new nation. It took great faith for Abraham to leave his country and wealth behind, travel to a land that he had never seen, and trust God for a son when he was 100 years old and his wife, Sarah, was 90. As a result of Abraham's faith and his obedience to make the journey God had commanded, the nation of Israel was born.

In the New Testament, the Apostle Paul made four missionary journeys over a span of nearly 16 years. These journeys are recorded in Acts. He visited such famous cities as Rome, Philippi, Ephesus, Corinth and Thessalonica. Just like Abraham, Paul's journeys had a spiritual focus. He often visited the churches he founded, encouraging believers in their faith. In cities where the Gospel had never been preached, he sought to establish new churches. As a prisoner, he even carried the message of Jesus Christ to the very heart of the Roman Empire, the city of Rome.

What were the results of Paul's obedience and the journeys he took? First, the Gospel was spread to every part of the known world. There was not a major city untouched by the ministry of Paul. Second, he established numerous churches to carry out the Great Commission given by our Lord in Matthew 28:19–20. Finally, God used this time in Paul's life to guide his writing of many books (epistles) in the New Testament. These journeys of Paul changed the world forever.

Another quest occurred in 1620. After 66 days at sea, in a space no larger than a volleyball court, the 102 passengers aboard the Mayflower finally reached America. These Pilgrims, as they were called, had journeyed across the Atlantic Ocean to establish a colony in Massachusetts. This difficult journey was not taken by professional sailors or merchants seeking the wealth of the New World. These were common people who were on a very different type of journey—a spiritual journey.

There were at least three reasons for the Pilgrim's journey to America. First, they sought freedom to worship God. As a result of their faith, many of them had been imprisoned in England. Many more had experienced persecution, while others had even been put to death.

Second, the Pilgrims were seeking a better environment for rearing their children. They had concluded that the wealth and evil examples in England were tempting their children away from the proper worship of God. The Pilgrims sought a place where their children would be removed from these temptations and could grow into godly citizens.

Finally, the Pilgrims made the journey to America in hopes of sharing the Gospel of Christ. They knew that the new colonies would be ideal places to establish new churches. Besides, they had heard about the Indians and wanted the opportunity to take the Gospel to them.

Although the Pilgrims' physical journey covered more than 5,000 miles of ocean, it was their faith that caused them to board the Mayflower. While many people today follow the Pilgrims' example of feasting at Thanksgiving, they often ignore the reason that the Pilgrims set aside this special day. It was to give thanks to God for all of the abundant blessings that He had bestowed upon them.

Have you ever thought of your life as a journey? Maybe you haven't traveled great distances since your birth, but you have begun the most exciting quest of all—your life's journey. In the years ahead, your journey may take you to foreign countries, or it may take you no farther than the cities surrounding where you presently live.

As you have already learned, you are facing more than a physical journey along the path of life. God is also challenging you to take a journey that we have called a *Character Quest*.

In the past few months, you have studied the following character traits: patience, integrity, forgiveness, initiative, contentment, encouragement, discernment, sincerity, purity, maturity, controlled speech, kindness, respect, leadership, commitment, service and reverence. Including what you may have previously learned in *Character Quest Volume 1*, your quest has already explored 34 different character traits.

As you continue your personal Character Quest, it is your responsibility to daily apply the lessons you have learned. Wherever your life's journey takes you, your character will be with you. If you desire to glorify God, experience joy and achieve success, then remember, CHARACTER MATTERS!

It is now time for you to continue your *Character Quest*. As you do, think about how the following words can encourage you along the way:

"Character is what you are in the dark."
(Dwight L. Moody)

"Happiness is not the end of life; character is."
(Henry Ward Beecher)

"We sow a thought and reap an act,
We sow an act and reap a habit,
We sow a habit and reap a character,
We sow a character and reap a destiny."
(William Makepeace Thackeray)

"I have walked in my integrity.
I have also trusted in the Lord."
(Psalm 26:1)

Inquiry-Action 36.1

Review It or Lose It!

Character trait: _____

Key verse: _____

Definition: _____
_____

Biblical example/story illustrating this character trait:
_____
_____

Three important facts I have learned about this character trait:
   1) _____

   2) _____

   3) _____

The main reason students do not demonstrate this character trait in their lives:
_____
_____

Example of how this character trait can be demonstrated in my life:
_____
_____

INQUIRY-ACTION 36.2

REVIEW IT OR LOSE IT!

Character trait: _____

Key verse: _____

Definition: _____

_____

Biblical example/story illustrating this character trait:

_____

_____

Three important facts I have learned about this character trait:

1) _____

2) _____

3) _____

The main reason students do not demonstrate this character trait in their lives:

_____

_____

Example of how this character trait can be demonstrated in my life:

_____

_____

Inquiry-Action 36.3

Final Commitment

Your paper will not be seen by anyone except you. Your honesty will allow God to work in you as you develop godly character.

- The one truth from this course that has been most important to me is:

  _____.

- A character trait which I feel confident in is:

  _____.

- The character trait that needs most improvement is:

  _____.

- The biggest obstacle to my improving this area is:

  _____.

- Some things I want to work on are:

  _____

  _____.

- I want to commit myself to developing godly character.   Yes ❑   No ❑
  If yes, complete the next page.

INQUIRY–ACTION 36.4

Commitment to Character

Based on the challenges presented in this course, I am willing to commit myself to the development of godly character. I understand that this includes both believing and doing the right things based on God's Word.

Signed: _____

Dated: _____

"I have walked in my integrity. I have also trusted in the Lord."
Psalm 26:1